NOW READ ON

A READING AND LANGUAGE PRACTICE
BOOK

T. U. SACHS

LONGMAN

LONGMAN GROUP LIMITED
London

*Associated companies, branches and representatives
throughout the world*

First published 1969
*New impressions *1970 (twice); *1971;*
*1972 (twice);*1974 ; *1975*

ISBN 0 582 52432 6

Printed in Hong Kong by
Peninsula Press Ltd

Contents

Contents

Acknowledgments

WE are grateful to the following for permission to reproduce copyright material and to adapt this where agreed:

George Allen & Unwin Ltd for extracts from 'How to Grow Old' by Bertrand Russell from *New Hopes for a Changing World*; author's agents for an extract from 'The Honest Man and the Devil' from *On Anything* by Hilaire Belloc; the Bodley Head and McClelland and Stewart Ltd for extracts from 'The Awful Fate of Melpomenus Jones' by Stephen Leacock from *Literary Lapses*; Jonathan Cape Ltd, The Society of Authors as the literary representative of the Estate of the late James Joyce, and The Viking Press Inc for 'Eveline' from *Dubliners* by James Joyce (originally published by B. W. Huebsch Inc in 1916, all rights reserved); Miss Collins and Sheed & Ward Ltd and author's agents for 'England and Caricature' from *Lunacy and Letters* by G. K. Chesterton; author's agents for 'The Reward' from *Jorkens Borrow Another Whisky* by Lord Dunsany; Hamish Hamilton Ltd for 'The Secret Life of Walter Mitty' from the *Thurber Carnival* by James Thurber; The Literary Executor of W. Somerset Maugham and William Heinemann for 'Home' by W. Somerset Maugham from *Cosmopolitans*; author's agents for 'At the Tailor's' from *Self-Selected Essays* by J. B. Priestley and for 'The Collection' by V. S. Pritchett from *Collected Stories*; author for 'Among the Dahlias' from *Among the Dahlias and other Stories* by William Sansom; author and author's agents for 'The Barber Whose Uncle Had His Head Bitten Off by a Circus Tiger' from *Best Stories of William Saroyan* by William Saroyan; author, author's agents and

Victor Gollancz for 'The Inspiration of Mr Budd' from *In the Teeth of the Evidence* by Dorothy L. Sayers; The Society of Authors as the literary representative of the Estate of the late Katherine Mansfield for 'The Singing Lesson' by Katherine Mansfield; author's agents for 'Bella Fleace Gave a Party' by Evelyn Waugh; and the Executors of H. G. Wells for 'The Truth about Pyecraft' from *Selected Stories* by H. G. Wells.

We are grateful to the following for permission to reproduce photographs on the cover:

Radio Times Hulton Picture Library for the photographs of James Joyce, G. K. Chesterton, Hilaire Belloc and Katherine Mansfield; Keystone Press Agency Ltd for the photograph of Dorothy Sayers; Karch for the photographs of H. G. Wells and Somerset Maugham; Camera Press Ltd for the photograph of Bertrand Russell.

Foreword

'Reading maketh a full man.'

FRANCIS BACON

READING a good story or essay is one of the most enjoyable – and therefore one of the best – roads for the explorer of a foreign language and of strange social and cultural climates. But the student at an intermediate level is often discouraged by the writer's idiosyncracies of style as well as by an apparently inordinate length of the text. Most of the 20 short stories and essays by well-known British and American authors in this book have therefore been abridged so as to permit a reasonably rapid first reading at one sitting or during one lesson, and the vocabulary has been slightly and unobtrusively simplified. The transition to completely unadapted prose should present no difficulty at the next stage.

Arbitrary as is the choice in any anthology, the criterion for the inclusion of a text was its readability and teachability: it is hoped that this book will provide reading enjoyment as well as an improvement in the student's language performance and some acquaintance with social and cultural settings in English-speaking countries.

This book is for students of the level of those who have completed the Cambridge Lower Certificate course and are beginning the study of works of literature such as those which are set for the Cambridge Proficiency Certificate.

The text is followed by a biographical note on the author, reading notes on points where help may be found useful, and by a set of exercises.

The notes explain difficulties, especially of phrase or structure, that cannot be solved by reference to a dictionary.

The exercises are designed to lead the student, as he works through them, to refer constantly to the text and in this way to get the fullest benefit from his reading of it.

Students working on their own without a teacher may, it is hoped, find the book particularly suited to their needs. In the classroom, the teacher should find the subjects for oral and written composition a stimulus to discussion and debate.

1

The Awful Fate of Melpomenus Jones

STEPHEN LEACOCK

SOME PEOPLE – not you nor I, because we are so awfully self-possessed – but some people, find great difficulty in saying good-bye when making a call or spending the evening. As the moment draws near when the visitor feels that he is fairly entitled to go away he rises and says suddenly, 'Well, I think I . . .' Then the people say, 'Oh, must you go now? Surely it's early yet!' and a pitiful struggle follows.

I think the saddest case of this kind of thing that I ever knew was that of my poor friend Melpomenus Jones, a clergyman – such a dear young man and only twenty-three! He 10 simply couldn't get away from people. He was too modest to tell a lie, and too religious to wish to appear rude. Now it happened that he went to call on some friends of his on the very first afternoon of his summer vacation. The next six weeks were entirely his own – absolutely nothing to do. He chattered a while, drank two cups of tea, then prepared himself for the effort and said suddenly:

'Well, I think I . . .'

But the lady of the house said, 'Oh, no! Mr Jones, can't you really stay a little longer?' 20

Jones was always truthful. 'Oh, yes,' he said, 'of course, I – er – can stay.'

'Then please don't go.'

He stayed. He drank eleven cups of tea. Night was falling. He rose again.

'Well now,' he said shyly, 'I think I really . . .'

'You must go?' said the lady politely. 'I thought perhaps you could have stayed to dinner . . .'

'Oh well, so I could, you know,' Jones said, 'if . . .'

30   'Then please stay, I'm sure my husband will be delighted.'

'All right,' he said feebly, 'I'll stay,' and he sank back into his chair, just full of tea and miserable.

Papa came home. They had dinner. All through the meal Jones sat planning to leave at eight-thirty. All the family wondered whether Mr Jones was stupid and ill-tempered, or only stupid.

After dinner mama tried to 'draw him out', and showed him photographs. She showed him all the family museum, several hundreds of them – photos of papa's uncle and his

40   wife, and mama's brother and his little boy, an awfully interesting photo of papa's uncle's friend in his Bengal uniform, an awfully well-taken photo of papa's grandfather's partner's dog, and an awfully wicked one of papa as the devil for a fancy-dress ball.

At eight-thirty Jones had examined seventy-one photographs.

There were about sixty-nine more that he hadn't. Jones rose. 'I must say good night now,' he pleaded.

'Say good night!' they said, 'why it's only half past eight! Have you anything to do?'

50   'Nothing,' he admitted, and muttered something about staying six weeks, and then laughed miserably.

Just then it turned out that the favourite child of the family, such a dear little boy, had hidden Mr Jones's hat; so papa said that he must stay, and invited him to a pipe and a chat. Papa had the pipe and gave Jones the chat, and still he stayed. Every moment he meant to take the plunge, but couldn't. Then papa began to get very tired of Jones and finally said, with irony, that Jones had better stay all night, they could make up a bed for him. Jones mistook his meaning

60   and thanked him with tears in his eyes, and papa put Jones to bed in the spare room and cursed him heartily.

After breakfast next day, papa went off to his work in the city, and left Jones playing with the baby, broken-hearted. His nerve was utterly gone. He was meaning to leave all day, but the thing had got on his mind and he simply couldn't. When papa came home in the evening he was surprised and angry to find Jones still there. He thought to get rid of him with a joke, and said he thought he'd have to charge him for his board, he! he! The unhappy young man stared wildly for a moment, then shook papa's hand, paid him a month's board in advance, and broke down and sobbed like a child.

In the days that followed he was moody and unapproachable. He lived, of course, entirely in the drawing-room, and the lack of air and exercise began to affect his health. He passed his time in drinking tea and looking at the photographs. He would stand for hours gazing at the photograph of papa's uncle's friend in his Bengal uniform – talking to it, sometimes swearing bitterly at it. His mind was obviously failing.

At length the crash came. They carried him upstairs in a raging delirium of fever. The illness that followed was terrible. He recognised no one, not even papa's uncle's friend in his Bengal uniform. At times he would start up from his bed and shriek, 'Well, I think I . . .' and then fall back upon the pillow with a horrible laugh. Then, again, he would jump up and cry, 'Another cup of tea and more photographs! More photographs! Har! Har!'

At length, after a month of agony, on the last day of his vacation, he passed away. They say that when the last moment came, he sat up in bed with a beautiful smile of confidence playing upon his face, and said, 'Well – the angels are calling me; I'm afraid I really must go now. Good afternoon.'

And the rushing of his spirit from its prison-house was as quick as a hunted cat passing over a garden fence.

THE AUTHOR

Stephen Leacock (1882–1944) was born in England. When he was seven years old, his parents emigrated to Canada. He was educated in Canada and in the United States, and is therefore to be considered as a North American writer.

He is well known to English-speaking people all over the world as a writer of humorous stories and essays, but he was not only a humorist. He was Professor of Economics and Political Science at McGill University, Toronto, Canada, and wrote an important text-book on political science. He also wrote studies of the works of Mark Twain, the nineteenth-century American humorist and author of *Tom Sawyer*, and of Charles Dickens, the English novelist who created many characters of world-wide fame such as Oliver Twist and Mr Pickwick. He is, however, best known for his own humorous writings, which are in some ways in the tradition of Mark Twain. Like Mark Twain, he gets some of his funniest effects by exaggerating some feature or other of real life, as in this story.

READING NOTES

The tone and incidents of this story give a Canadian's idea of life in a certain section of English society forty or fifty years ago.

Line 1 *awfully:* very. *Awfully* is used in this way in colloquial conversation by the kind of people whose conversation is full of exaggeration. There is a similar example in lines 10–11 – 'He simply couldn't get away from people.'

3 *making a call:* paying a visit. Notice the change of verb if we use 'visit'.

4 *fairly*. *Fairly* is often used as an adverb of degree (e.g. 'fairly warm', which means 'quite warm' but is less strong than 'very warm'). Here, however, it has a totally different meaning. It is the corresponding adverb to 'fair' meaning 'just' or 'right'. The whole phrase means that the visitor has stayed long enough, and that he now has the right to leave. The point of the story depends very much on the humorous suggestion that calling on people is a social obligation rather than a pleasure.

7 *a pitiful struggle*. Leacock imagines that both the host and the guest are anxious to put an end to the visit, but that each of them

is so polite that he does not want to take the first step in doing so.

22 *er*. This represents a sound made by nervous people, when they are hesitating over what to say next.

27–8 The key to the rest of the story is here. The hostess, not wishing to appear rude, says something that she does not really mean – 'I thought you could have stayed to dinner.' Mr Jones, who has no other engagement, cannot tell a lie and accepts the invitation, though his acceptance pleases neither of them. That is why we are told in line 32 that he sank back into his chair, 'miserable'.

35 Mr Jones was not ill-tempered, but silent because he was worried about not being able to get away.

37 *draw him out:* get him to talk, get him interested.

41 *in his Bengal uniform.* This phrase tells us at what period this story happened, namely in the early years of the twentieth century, the period known as 'Edwardian' because Edward VII was king of England. The army was one of the professions which the sons of wealthy people entered at that time, and many of them served in India. The man in this photograph had evidently been an officer in a regiment in Bengal, perhaps the famous Bengal Lancers.

47 *pleaded:* begged. Suggests that the unfortunate Mr Jones was asking for permission to go away.

55 *Papa had the pipe and gave Jones the chat.* Papa smoked and did all the talking as well. We may imagine that a delicate young clergyman like Mr Jones would dislike the smell of tobacco smoke, and would also dislike having to listen to a lot of talk when he really wanted to get away.

56 *take the plunge:* take a sudden and bold decision. Literally the expression means 'dive into water'; it is commonly used to suggest that the water is very deep or cold.

58 *with irony*. These words indicate one more misunderstanding between Jones and his hosts.

61 *heartily*. This word usually means 'cheerfully', but here it suggests that Papa relieved his angry feelings by cursing Jones very strongly.

63 *broken-hearted*. Jones, of course, not the baby.

64 *nerve*. A common use of this word to mean 'courage'.

69 *board*. This means the cost of food. Compare 'board and lodging', which means that food and accommodation are provided, 'Boarding school' and 'boarder' (a boarder being a person who lives and has his or her meals in a boarding establishment).

EXERCISES

A. Answer these questions.

1. What is the 'pitiful struggle' mentioned in the first paragraph of the story?
2. What are we told in the second paragraph about Mr Jones's character?
3. 'You must go?' said the lady politely. 'I thought perhaps you could have stayed to dinner . . .' What did the hostess really intend by these words, and what was their effect on Jones?
4. 'He thought to get rid of him with a joke . . .' Why did this plan fail?
5. What happened during Jones's last moments?

B. Show the meaning of these expressions by using them in sentences.

board (*n*)	fancy dress	chatter (*v*)
chat (*n*)	spare room	sob (*v*)
curse (*v*)	unapproachable	
plead	vacation	

C. Find expressions in the story with the same meaning as those below:

1. make up one's mind and take action
2. he was losing his sanity
3. he had nothing to do for the next six weeks
4. send him away
5. a disaster happened
6. to say what is not true
7. it was discovered that . . .
8. he had lost his courage
9. he lost his self-control
10. sarcastically

D. Give the correct form of the verb in brackets in each of these sentences.

1. Some people find difficulty in (say) good-bye.
2. Mr Jones was too modest (tell) a lie.
3. He had absolutely nothing (do).
4. He spent an hour (look) at photographs.
5. He muttered something about (stay) six weeks.
6. Papa said he had better (stay) all night.
7. He left Jones (play) with the baby.
8. Jones was meaning (leave) every day.
9. Papa was angry (find) Jones still there.
10. The lack of exercise began (affect) his health.

E. Change each sentence by giving an adverb instead of the adjective in italics and a suitable verb instead of the noun in italics, and make any other necessary alterations.

Example
Jones gave a *cold stare* at his hostess.
Jones stared coldly at his hostess.

1. Jones made a *pitiful struggle* to get away.
2. He gave a *nervous smile* when his hostess asked him to dinner.
3. He made *feeble comments* on the photographs.
4. He gave a *miserable laugh* and sat down.
5. Papa uttered a *hearty curse* after he had put Jones to bed.
6. In the days that followed, Jones's *behaviour* was *moody*.
7. Jones uttered a *horrible laugh* as he fell back on the pillow.
8. He had a *confident smile* as he sat up in bed.
9. The hunted cat made a *quick rush* over a garden fence.
10. He never made an *untruthful speech*, not even to save his life.

F. Write out this passage with the verbs in brackets in their proper forms.

Jones (mistake) his meaning and (thank) him with tears in his eyes, and Papa (put) Jones to bed in the spare room and (curse) him heartily. After breakfast next day, Papa (go) off to his work in the city and (leave) Jones (play) with the baby, broken-hearted. He (mean, leave) all day, but the thing (get) on his mind and he simply (can, *negative*). When Papa (come) home in the evening he (be) surprised and angry (find) Jones still there.

G. Subjects for composition and discussion:
   1. Give examples of exaggeration in the story which produce a humorous effect.
   2. 'Some people – not you nor I . . .' Do you know any 'Joneses'? Do you sympathise more with them or with the people they visit?
   3. Imagine you are the lady of the house. Write to your mother, telling her all about Mr Jones's visit.

2

Eveline

JAMES JOYCE

SHE sat at the window watching the evening enter the avenue. Her head was leaned against the window curtains, and in her nostrils was the odour of dusty cotton cloth. She was tired.

Few people passed. The man out of the last house passed on his way home; she heard his footsteps clacking along the concrete pavement and afterwards crunching on the path before the new red houses. Once there used to be a field there in which they used to play every evening with other people's children. Then a man from Belfast bought the field and built houses on it – not like their little brown houses, but bright 10 brick houses with shining roofs. The children of the avenue used to play together in that field – the Devines, the Waters, the Dunns, little Keogh the cripple, she and her brothers and sisters. Ernest, however, never played: he was too grown up. Her father used often to hunt them in out of the field with his blackthorn stick. Still they seemed to have been rather happy then. Her father was not so bad then; and besides, her mother was alive. That was a long time ago; she and her brothers and sisters were all grown up; her mother was dead. Tizzie Dunn was dead, too, and the Waters had gone back to England. 20 Everything changes. Now she was going to go away like the others, to leave her home.

Home! She looked round the room, reviewing all its familiar objects which she had dusted once a week for so many years, wondering where on earth all the dust came from. Perhaps she would never see again those familiar objects from which she had never dreamed of being divided.

She had consented to go away, to leave her home. Was that
wise? She tried to weigh each side of the question. In her home
30   anyway she had shelter and food; she had those whom she had
known all her life about her. Of course she had to work hard,
both in the house and at business. What would they say of her
at the Stores when they found out that she had run away with
a fellow? Say she was a fool, perhaps; and her place would be
filled up by advertisement. Miss Gavan would be glad. She had
always spoken harshly to her, especially whenever there were
people listening.

'Miss Hill, don't you see these ladies are waiting?'

'Look lively, Miss Hill, please.'

40   She would not cry many tears at leaving the Stores.

But in her new home, in a distant unknown country, it
would not be like that. Then she would be married – she,
Eveline. People would treat her with respect then. She would
not be treated as her mother had been. Even now, though she
was over nineteen, she sometimes felt herself in danger of her
father's violence. She knew it was that that had given her the
palpitations. When they were growing up he had never struck
her, as he used to strike Harry and Ernest, because she was a
girl; but lately he had begun to threaten her and say what he
50   would do to her only for her dead mother's sake. And now she
had nobody to protect her. Ernest was dead and Harry, who
was in the church decorating business, was nearly always
down somewhere in the country. Besides, the invariable
quarrel about money on Saturday nights had begun to weary
her unspeakably. She always gave her entire wages – seven
shillings – and Harry always sent up what he could, but the
trouble was to get any money from her father. He said she
used to waste the money, that she had no head, that he
wasn't going to give her his hard-earned money to throw about
60   the streets, and much more, for he was usually fairly bad on
Saturday night. In the end he would give her the money and
ask her had she any intention of buying Sunday's dinner.
Then she had to rush out as quickly as she could and do her

marketing, holding her black leather purse tightly in her hand as she elbowed her way through the crowds and returning home late under her load of provisions. She had hard work to keep the house together and see that the two young children who had been left to her charge went to school regularly and got their meals regularly. It was hard work – a hard life – but now that she was about to leave it she did not find it a wholly undesirable life. 70

She was about to explore another life with Frank. Frank was very kind, manly, open-hearted. She was to go away with him by the night-boat to be his wife and to live with him in Buenos Ayres, where he had a home waiting for her. How well she remembered the first time she had seen him! He was lodging in a house on the main road where she used to visit. It seemed a few weeks ago. He was standing at the gate, his cap pushed on his head and his hair tumbled forward over a face of bronze. Then they had come to know each other. He 80 used to meet her outside the Stores every evening and see her home. He took her to see *The Bohemian Girl* and she felt excited as she sat in an unaccustomed part of the theatre with him. He was awfully fond of music and sang a little. People knew that they were courting, and, when he sang about the lass that loves a sailor, she always felt pleasantly confused. First of all it had been an excitement for her to have a fellow and then she had begun to like him. He told tales of distant countries. He had started as a deck boy at a pound a month on a ship of the Allan Line going out to Canada. He told her the 90 names of the ships he had been on and the names of the different services. He had fallen on his feet in Buenos Ayres, he said, and had come over to the old country just for a holiday. Of course, her father had found out the affair and had forbidden her to have anything to say to him.

'I know these sailor chaps,' he said.

One day he had quarrelled with Frank, and after that she had to meet her lover secretly.

The evening deepened in the avenue. The white of two

100 letters in her lap grew indistinct. One was to Harry; the other
was to her father. Ernest had been her favourite, but she liked
Harry too. Her father was becoming old lately, she noticed;
he would miss her. Sometimes he could be very nice. Not long
before, when she had been laid up for a day, he had read her
out a ghost story and made toast for her at the fire. Another
day, when their mother was alive, they had all gone for a
picnic to the Hill of Howth. She remembered her father putting on her mother's hat to make the children laugh.

Her time was running out, but she continued to sit by the
110 window, leaning her head against the window curtain, in-
haling the odour of dusty cotton cloth. Down in the avenue
she could hear a street organ playing. She knew the tune.
Strange that it should come that very night to remind her of
the promise to her mother, her promise to keep the home together as long as she could. She remembered the last night of
her mother's illness; she was again in the close, dark room at
the other side of the hall and outside she heard a melancholy
tune of Italy. The organ-player had been ordered to go away
and been given sixpence. She remembered her father walking
120 back into the sick-room saying:

'Damned Italians! Coming over here!'

As she mused the pitiful vision of her mother's life laid its
spell on her very soul – that life of common-place sacrifices
ending in final craziness. She trembled as she heard again her
mother's voice saying constantly with foolish insistence:

'Derevaun Seraun! Derevaun Seraun!'

She stood up in a sudden impulse of terror. Escape! She must
escape! Frank would save her. He would give her life, perhaps
love, too. But she wanted to live. Why should she be unhappy?
150 She had a right to happiness. Frank would take her in his arms,
fold her in his arms. He would save her.

. . . .

She stood among the swaying crowd in the station at the
North Wall. He held her hand and she knew that he was

speaking to her, saying something about the passage over and over again. The station was full of soldiers with brown baggages. Through the wide doors of the sheds she caught a glimpse of the black mass of the boat, lying beside the quay wall, with lighted portholes. She answered nothing. She felt her cheek pale and cold and, out of a confusion of pain, she 140 prayed to God to direct her, to show her what was her duty. The boat blew a long mournful whistle into the mist. If she went, to-morrow she would be on the sea with Frank, steaming towards Buenos Ayres. Their passage had been booked. Could she still draw back after all he had done for her? Her pain awoke a nausea in her body and she kept moving her lips in silent fervent prayer.

A bell clanged upon her heart. She felt him seize her hand:
'Come!'

All the seas of the world tumbled about her heart. He was 150 drawing her into them: he would drown her. She gripped with both hands at the iron railing.

'Come!'

No! No! No! It was impossible. Her hands clutched the iron in madness. Amid the seas she sent a cry of anguish.

'Eveline! Evvy!'

He rushed beyond the barrier and called to her to follow. He was shouted at to go on, but he still called to her. She set her white face to him, passive, like a helpless animal. Her eyes gave him no sign of love or farewell or recognition.   160

THE AUTHOR

James Joyce (1882–1941) was born in Dublin, now the capital of the Irish Republic, but spent most of his grown-up life in France and other Continental countries. His work has had a great influence on many modern English writers. *Eveline* is taken from an early book of short stories called *Dubliners* which describes the lives of people in Dublin. James also wrote two well-known novels. The first of these, *Portrait of the Artist as a Young Man*, is about his

own early life. The other, *Ulysses*, which is also about life in
Dublin, is his best-known work. *Ulysses* and Joyce's last book,
Finnegan's Wake, still arouse a great deal of discussion in literary
circles.

READING NOTES

Ireland is a poor country, and for many years Irish people have
emigrated to other lands, especially the American continent, to
seek a better living than they could hope for at home. This is the
background to *Eveline*.

Line 2 Her head was leaned. It would be more usual to say 'She
was leaning her head'.

4 *few:* not many. Do not confuse it with 'a few', which means
'some'.

5-6 *clacking, crunching.* These words describe the different sounds
made by the man's feet as he walked first along the hard concrete
pavement and then on a soft gravel path.

10 *brown houses.* Brown because they were built of brown stone,
which had a soft colour. The brick of the new houses was bright
red, and contrasted with it.

15 *hunt.* This suggests that their father threatened them with his
stick to make them go into the house.

16 *Still.* This marks a contrast with the previous sentence. It
means 'nevertheless' or 'in spite of that'.

21 *Everything changes.* The present tense is used here because the
writer is saying something that is always true.

23 *reviewing.* Not only looking at, but thinking about, the objects
in the room.

29 *weigh:* consider carefully. *Weigh* is used in this sense particularly when opposite points of view are being considered.

30 *anyway:* at least.

33 *Stores.* A capital letter is used because this is the name of a
particular shop where Eveline worked.

34 *a fellow.* This is a colloquial use of *fellow* to mean a man with
whom a girl is in love.

39 *Look lively:* 'be quick'.

40 *cry many tears.* It would be more usual to say 'shed many
tears'. This is a colloquial Irish usage.

47 *palpitations:* violent beatings of the heart, in this case caused by fear.

50 *only for:* but for, or except for.

55 *unspeakably.* The quarrels about money worried her so much that she could not bear to speak about them.

58 *she had no head:* she was not careful with money.

65 *elbowed:* pushed through the crowds by using her elbows.

75 *Buenos Ayres.* This is now spelt 'Buenos Aires' in English.

79 *tumbled.* This past participle matches 'pushed' in the same line. It would be more usual to say 'tumbling'.

82 *The Bohemian Girl.* A light opera about gipsy life by a nineteenth-century Irish composer, Joaquim Balfe.

85 *courting:* associating with someone with a view to getting married.

92 *He had fallen on his feet:* He had managed to make a good living, or He had been lucky.

93 *the old country:* the country where he was born.

96 *these sailor chaps. Chaps* is a colloquial word for men. It suggests here that Eveline's father did not trust sailors.

99–100 *The white of two letters . . . indistinct.* A vivid way of describing how it grew dark as Eveline sat there.

103 *miss her:* be sorry she had gone away.

104 *laid up:* ill in bed.

112 *street organ.* Better known in English as 'barrel organ', this instrument on wheels was pushed along by street musicians and played tunes when they turned a handle.

126 *Derevaun Seraun.* These two words, apparently Irish, do not in fact mean anything.

131 *fold her in his arms:* embrace her, or protect her.

135 *passage:* sea journey, voyage.

137 *baggages.* 'Baggage', like 'luggage', is generally used only in the singular. The plural here gives an idea of a great quantity of baggage.

139 *portholes.* The windows in a ship, usually round.

143–4 *steaming:* travelling in a steamship.

146 *pain:* sorrow,

nausea: a feeling of sickness, in this case caused by strong emotion.

148 *A bell clanged upon her heart.* A bell rang to warn passengers

that the ship was about to leave, and its sound made Eveline
agitated, because she knew that she must decide now whether
to go or not.

155 *amid:* among, used normally only in poetry.

158 *He was shouted at.* He was shouted at by the crew of the
ship, to warn him that he must go on board.

   set: turned, but in a fixed, motionless position, because she
was seized by powerful emotions which made her unable to take
any decision.

EXERCISES

A. Answer these questions.

   1. What were the circumstances of Eveline's life that had
      changed?
   2. 'Her father was not so bad then.' 'He was usually bad
      on Saturday nights.' What do these remarks suggest to
      you?
   3. 'It was hard work.' Describe Eveline's work at home
      and at the Stores.
   4. What facts about Frank have you learnt from the
      story?
   5. 'He would save her.' (131). 'He would drown her.' (151)
      Explain this change in Eveline's thoughts about Frank.

B. Use each of these words in a sentence, to show that you
understand its meaning:

   anguish   fervent   invariable   melancholy   provisions
   cripple (*n*) inhale lodge (*v*)   odour   review (*v*)

C. Find expressions in the story with the same meaning as
those below:

   1. She could smell dusty   5. He used to walk home
      cotton cloth.   with her.
   2. Hurry up.   6. The avenue grew dark.
   3. To spend foolishly.   7. She had not much time
   4. Left in her care.   left.

8. To prevent the family from breaking up.

9. (The memory of her mother) held her as if by the power of magic.

10. She had a quick sight of the boat.

D. Put in the missing prepositions or adverbs.

1. She had consented to go . . .
2. She had to work hard both . . . the house and . . . business.
3. What would they say . . . her . . . the Stores when they found . . . that she had run . . . . . . a fellow?
4. Her place would be filled . . . advertisement.
5. Miss Gavan had always spoken harshly . . . her.
6. She would not cry many tears . . . leaving the Stores.
7. But . . . her new home, . . . a distant country, people would treat her . . . respect.
8. She had sometimes felt herself . . . danger . . . her father's violence.
9. Lately he had begun . . . threaten her.
10. When they were growing . . . he had never attacked her, only . . . her mother's sake.

E. The words in italics in (*a*) express a future meaning. Those in (*b*) express a past meaning. Make up two more examples of each kind of sentence.

   (*a*) She was *about to* explore another life.
   She was *to* go away with him.

   (*b*) She *used to* play there.
   Miss Gavan *had always* spoken harshly to her.

F. Rewrite the sentences below, using the correct form of one of these expressions:

   call, call for, call in at, call on, call up, make calls.
   1. Mr Jones visited some friends while he was on holiday.

2. What name are you going to give your new baby?
3. The sailors shouted out to Frank to go on board.
4. I have done nothing but speak on the telephone all morning.
5. I want you to go to the post office and buy some stamps on your way home.
6. The doctor paid several visits during the morning.
7. If you find your work too hard, you can always ask me to help you.
8. My friends are going to fetch me in their car.
9. If war breaks out, all the men will be sent for to join the army.
10. Shy people don't like paying visits, because they don't know how to say good-bye.

G. Subjects for composition and discussion:

1. 'Eveline did her duty.'
   'Eveline was a coward.'
   Which of these statements is more true? Give reasons for your answer.
2. Show how the writer prepares the reader during the story for Eveline's behaviour at the end.

3

At the Tailor's

J. B. PRIESTLEY

BETWEEN Regent Street and New Bond Street is a little
region that is curiously quiet. It does not seem as if anything
is being sold in this part of the world. Whatever the season, no
Sales are held there. You are not invited to stop a moment
longer than you may wish to do. Now and then you catch sight
of a roll of cloth, a pair of riding breeches, or, perhaps, a single
little drawing of a gentleman in evening clothes, and as you
pass you can hear these things whispering: 'If you are a gentleman and wish to wear the clothes that a gentleman should
wear, kindly make an appointment here and we will see what   10
we can do for you.' Money, of course, is not mentioned, this
being impossible in all such gentlemanly business. For this is
the region, Savile Row, Conduit Street, Maddox Street, and
the rest, of the tailors or – rather – *the* tailors. Enter it wearing
a cheap ready-made suit, and immediately the poor thing
begins to bag in some places and become wrinkled in others.
If you dare (as I once did) actually to walk into one of these
establishments wearing a ready-made suit, you will regret it.
Nothing is said, but a glance from one of the higher officials
here strips you and quietly places your suit in the dustbin.   20
     The quiet here is significant. It might be described as old-
world, and for a very good reason, too. In a new world in which
anything will do so long as it arrives quickly and easily, this
region is now sadly behind the times. Tailoring here remains
one of the arts. That these tailors are artists and not tradesmen
is proved by the fact that, unlike tradesmen, they do not labour
to please their customers, but to please themselves. A tailor

who is a mere shopkeeper fits you until you are satisfied. These artists go on fitting you until they are satisfied, and that means they continue long after you have lost all interest in the matter. You stand there, a mere body or figure, and they still go on delicately tearing out sleeves and collars with their little penknives, pinning and unpinning, and making signs with chalk, and you have long ceased to understand what all the bother is about. And even then they may tell you, quietly but firmly, that they must have another fitting. That they should do this to me is proof of their disinterested passion for the art of tailoring.

I never walk into my own tailor's without feeling apologetic. I know I am unworthy of their efforts. It is as if a man without an ear for music should be invited to spend an evening with the Lener Quartet. I am the kind of man who can make any suit of clothes look shabby and undistinguished after about a fort-night's wear. Perhaps the fact that I always carry about with me two or three fairly large pipes, matches, about two ounces of tobacco, a wallet, cheque-book, diary, fountain-pen, knife, odd keys and loose change, to say nothing of old letters, may have something to do with it. I can never understand how a man can manage to look neat and smart and do anything else. Wearing clothes properly seems to me to be a full-time job, and as I happen to have a great many other more important or more amusing things to do, I cheerfully bag and sag and look as if I had slept in my suits. I can say this cheerfully here, but once I am inside my tailor's I immediately begin to feel apologetic. They do not say anything, but there is mournful reproach in their eyes as they turn them upon their ruined sonnets and sonatas.

They have their revenge, though, when they get me inside one of their horrible cubicles for a fitting. By the time I have been inside one of those places ten minutes I have not a bit of self-respect left. It is worse than being at the barber's, and fully equal to being at the dentist's. To stand like a dummy, to be simply a shape of flesh and bone, is bad enough, but what makes it much worse are the mirrors and the lighting. These mirrors go shining away endlessly. I do not like all those images of myself. Wherever I look, I see a man whose appearance does not please me. His head seems rather too big for his body, his body rather too big for his legs. In that merciless bright light, his face looks fattish and heavy. There is something vaguely dirty about him. The clothes he is wearing, 70 apart from the particular garment he is trying on at the moment, look baggy, wrinkled, and shabby. He does not pay enough attention to his collar, his boots. His hair needs cutting, and another and closer shave would do him good. In full face he does not inspire confidence. His profile, however, is simply ridiculous, and the back view of him is really horrible. And a woman and several children are tied to a fellow like that! Incredible that a man can take such a face and body about with him, and yet have a fairly good opinion of himself! As I think these things, it is possible that I smile a little. That is 80 what it feels like – smiling a little; but immediately twenty images in that cubicle break into horrible grins, produce wrinkles from nowhere, show distorted acres of cheek and jowl. And there is no looking away.

Meanwhile, the tailors themselves, so neat, so clean, so skilful, are busy with the pins and the chalk. They are at home in these little halls of mirrors, and so look well in them from every possible angle of reflection. They are not all alike, these fitters, or cutters, or whatever they are. Thus my usual trouser man is quite different from my usual coat man. He is 90 smaller and livelier, more full of cheerful gossip. A long and intimate acquaintance with trousers has made him far more democratic and earthy. There are times when I feel I am almost a match for him. On the other hand the coat man is quietly wonderful. Everything about him is clear, polished, and perfect. He regards me with about the same amount of interest that I give to another man's coat. When he once was good enough to tell me about his boy (who is at a public school) I felt immensely flattered and rushed to agree with everything

100 he said. For a few minutes I was really alive, almost sharing the honours with my coat. But then he became serious again and took out a pin somewhere and made another chalkmark.

Now that the dandies are all dead and gone, it must be a lonely world for these artists. Will they accept these few words of tribute from a pocket-stuffer, a rumpler and wrinkler, a bagger?

THE AUTHOR

J. B. Priestley (b. 1894) was born in Bradford in West Yorkshire, one of the biggest industrial areas in northern England. After studying at Cambridge University, he worked in London as a journalist and reviewer. He made his name widely known by a novel, *The Good Companions*. This novel describes the romantic adventures of a practical Yorkshire carpenter with a travelling theatrical company. Priestley has written a number of plays, in which he is particularly interested in experiments with time, looking both to the past and to the future. Other works by him are a series of essays which give lively descriptions of aspects and scenes of contemporary life. These essays may be compared to the *Sketches by Boz* of Charles Dickens, written more than a century ago; but Dickens was interested above all in social aspects of life, whilst Priestley describes people at work. He is also well known as a frank and vigorous radio speaker on current affairs.

READING NOTES

At the Tailor's is one of Priestley's descriptions of people at work. In it he shows a humorous appreciation of that typically English institution, the London tailor's.

Line 1 *Regent Street and New Bond Street.* Streets of shops in the fashionable West End of London.

2 *curiously quiet:* strangely quiet. Strangely, because the streets round this region are noisy and full of traffic.

4 *Sales.* With a capital letter, this word means the bargain sales which shops hold at certain times of the year to attract people in search of goods at reduced prices.

7 *gentleman.* This word is repeated two or three times, and *gentlemanly* also occurs. Priestley wants us to feel the particular social atmosphere of these expensive tailors' shops.

14 THE *tailors.* Emphasised in this way (and pronounced (ði:), *the* means 'the best of their kind'.

15 *the poor thing:* the cheap ready-made suit.

16 *bag*: hang loosely, like a bag. Used as a verb to describe badly-fitting clothes.

19 *the higher officials.* These dignified tailors seem more like government employees than tradesmen.

21–2 *old-world:* old-fashioned.

23 *will do:* is good enough.

36 *fitting.* A trial of the suit before it is finally made up.

37 *disinterested.* Notice the difference in meaning between *disinterested* and *uninterested. Uninterested* means 'not taking any interest'. A disinterested person may take a great deal of interest in what he is doing, as these tailors do, but he is acting for unselfish reasons.

39 *tailor's:* tailor's shop.

42 *the Lener Quartet.* A well-known Hungarian string quartet, founded in 1920.

47 *odd keys:* keys carried about for no special reason.

47–8 *may have something to do with it.* This is a humorous understatement. Priestley knows that the great quantity of things which he carries in his pockets are the cause of the shabbiness of his suits, but he wants us to imagine him as a person who can never really understand why he looks badly dressed.

52 *I bag and sag:* my suits bag and sag.

56–7 *their ruined sonnets and sonatas.* A sonnet is a kind of poem. A sonata is a kind of musical composition. The tailors are seen as artists, though they express themselves in clothes and not in poetry or music.

62 *dummy.* A tailor's dummy is a model figure on which clothes are made up. In colloquial English, *dummy* also means a silly person who cannot do anything for himself.

65 *go shining away:* reflect each other endlessly.

69 *fattish:* rather fat. *-ish* is often added to adjectives in this way in colloquial English.

71 *apart from:* except for.

74 *in full face*. This contrasts with *profile* in the next sentence.

77 *are tied to:* depend on (because he is a husband and father).

84 *jowl.* An uncomplimentary word for a person's jaw, suggesting a heavy chin and a fat neck.

there is no looking away. He cannot avoid looking at himself, because he is surrounded by mirrors.

87 *so:* therefore.

90 *trouser man, coat man.* The tailor's assistants who specialise in trousers and coats.

93 *earthy:* down to earth, practical. Trousers are our lower garments, and so they are imagined here to be less dignified than coats.

94 *a match for:* as good as.

96-7 *the same amount of interest . . . another man's coat.* The tailor is interested only in the coat, not in the man for whom he is making it. Priestley is not interested in his own clothes, so he is not likely to take an interest in those of anyone else.

98 *at a public school.* This emphasises the desire of the coat man to be a gentleman. To go to a public school, which is in fact an expensive type of private school, is considered in some sections of English society as a mark of social distinction.

103 *dandies.* Men, especially in the eighteenth and early nineteenth centuries, whose principal interest was in being fashionably dressed.

105 *tribute:* praise.

EXERCISES

A. Answer these questions.

1. What would you notice if you visited the district of the tailors?
2. 'Tailoring here remains one of the arts.' What makes Priestley think so?
3. Why does Priestley feel apologetic when he visits his tailor's?
4. How does he look in the tailor's mirrors?
5. Why does he dislike going for a fitting?

6. What is the difference between the personalities of the trouser man and the coat man?

B. Find expressions in the story with the same meaning as those below:

1. a meeting at a fixed time
2. a suit not made to a customer's requirements
3. old-fashioned
4. coins in one's pocket
5. a rubbish container
6. unable to enjoy music
7. ordinary, common
8. a regular occupation
9. a small compartment in a room
10. a good opinion of oneself

C. Imagine that you heard Priestley say the passage which follows, and that you are reporting it for a newspaper. Begin with the words 'Priestley said that . . .' and write the passage again in indirect speech, making necessary changes of tense:

The quiet here is significant. It might be described as old-world, and for a very good reason, too. In a new world in which anything will do so long as it arrives quickly and easily, this region is now sadly behind the times. Tailoring here remains one of the arts. That these tailors are artists and not tradesmen is proved by the fact that, unlike tradesmen, they do not labour to please their customers, but to please themselves. A tailor who is a mere shopkeeper fits you until you are satisfied. These artists go on fitting you until they are satisfied, and that means they continue long after you have lost all interest in the matter.

D. Make two sentences for each of these words, using it first as a noun and then as a verb:

bag, glance, interest, labour, place

E. Make a sentence for each of these expressions, using it in the sense given after it in brackets:

1. fit for (suitable for)
2. fit (be the right shape and size)

N R O—B

3. a fit (the right shape and size)
4. a fit (a sudden convulsion or attack, e.g. of coughing)

F. In each of the sentences below, use in the proper position the most suitable of these adverbs: *delicately*, *immediately*, *immensely*, *properly*, *quietly*.

1. A glance from one of the higher officials places your suit in the dustbin.
2. They go on tearing out sleeves with their little pen-knives.
3. Wearing clothes seems to me to be a full-time job.
4. Once I was inside my tailor's I began to feel apologetic.
5. When he once told me about his boy I felt flattered.

G. Subjects for composition and discussion:

1. Priestley makes fun of the tailors, but he admires them. What does he admire them for?
2. Describe the personality of Priestley as he appears in this essay.
3. An English proverb says 'Clothes don't make a man.' How important do you think clothes are in our lives?

4

Home

W. SOMERSET MAUGHAM

THE farm lay in a small valley among the Somersetshire hills, an old-fashioned stone house surrounded by barns and pens and out-houses. Over the doorway the date when it was built had been carved in the elegant figures of the period, 1673, and the house, grey and weather-beaten, looked as much a part of the landscape as the trees that surrounded it. An avenue of splendid elms led from the road to the neat garden. The people who lived here were as unexcitable, strong and modest as the house; their only boast was that ever since it was built they had been born and died in it: from father to son in ·one un- 10 broken line. For three hundred years they had farmed the surrounding land. George Meadows was now a man of fifty, and his wife was a year or two younger. They were both fine, honest people in the prime of life; and their children, two sons and three girls, were handsome and strong. I have never seen a more united household. They were merry, industrious and kindly. Their life had a completeness that gave it a beauty as definite as that of a symphony of Beethoven's or a picture by Titian. They were happy and they deserved their happiness. But the master of the house was not George 20 Meadows (not by a long chalk, they said in the village); it was his mother. She was twice the man her son was, they said. She was a woman of seventy, tall, upright and dignified, with grey hair, and though her face was much wrinkled, her eyes were bright and shrewd. Her word was law in the house and on the farm; but she had humour, and if her rule was despotic it was also kindly. People laughed at her jokes and repeated them. She was a good business woman. She combined in a rare degree good will with a sense of the ridiculous. She was a character.

30   One day Mrs George stopped me on my way home. She was really excited. (Her mother-in-law was the only 'Mrs Meadows' we knew; George's wife was only known as 'Mrs George'.)

'Who ever do you think is coming here today?' she asked me. 'Uncle George Meadows. You know, he was in China.'

'Why, I thought he was dead.'

'We all thought he was dead.'

I had heard the story of Uncle George Meadows a dozen times, and it had amused me because it sounded like an old ballad: it was quite moving to come across it in real life. For

40   Uncle George Meadows and Tom, his younger brother, had both courted Mrs Meadows when she was Emily Green, fifty years and more ago, and when she married Tom, George had gone away to sea.

They heard of him on the China coast. For twenty years now and then he had sent them presents; then there was no more news of him; when Tom Meadows died his widow wrote and told him, but received no answer; and at last they came to the conclusion that he must be dead. But two or three days ago to their astonishment they had received a letter from

50   the matron of the sailors' home at Portsmouth. It appeared that for the last ten years George Meadows, crippled with rheumatism, had lived there, and now, feeling that he had not much longer to live, wanted to see once more the house in which he was born. Albert Meadows, his great-nephew, had gone over to Portsmouth in the Ford to fetch him and he was to arrive that afternoon.

'Just fancy,' said Mrs George, 'he's not been here for more than fifty years. He's never even seen my George, who's fifty-one next birthday.'

60   'And what does Mrs Meadows think of it?' I asked.

'Well, you know what she is. She sits there and smiles to herself. All she says is, "He was a good-looking young fellow when he left, but not so steady as his brother," That's why she chose my George's father. "But he's probably quietened down by now," she says.'

Mrs George asked me to look in and see him. With the simplicity of a country woman who had never been further from her home than London, she thought that because we had both been in China we must have something in common. Of course I accepted. I found the whole family assembled when I arrived; they were sitting in the great old kitchen, with its stone floor, Mrs Meadows in her usual chair by the fire, very upright, and I was amused to see that she had put on her best silk dress, while her son and his wife sat at the table with their children. On the other side of the fireplace sat an old man, bunched up in a chair. He was very thin and his skin hung on his bones like an old suit much too large for him; his face was wrinkled and yellow and he had lost nearly all his teeth.

I shook hands with him.

'Well, I'm glad to see you've got here safely, Mr Meadows,' I said.

'Captain,' he corrected.

'He walked here,' Albert, his great-nephew, told me. 'When he got to the gate he made me stop the car and said he wanted to walk.'

'And mind you, I've not been out of my bed for two years. They carried me down and put me in the car. I thought I'd never walk again, but when I saw those elm trees, I felt I could walk. I walked down that drive fifty-two years ago when I went away and now I've walked back again.'

'Silly, I call it,' said Mrs Meadows.

'It's done me good. I feel better and stronger than I have for ten years. I'll see you out yet, Emily.'

'Don't you be too sure,' she answered.

I suppose no one had called Mrs Meadows by her first name for a generation. It gave me a little shock, as though the old man were taking a liberty with her. She looked at him with a shrewd smile in her eyes and he, talking to her, grinned with his toothless gums. It was strange to look at them, these two

100 old people who had not seen one another for half a century,
and to think that all that long time ago he had loved her and
she had loved another. I wondered if they remembered what
they had felt then and what they had said to one another. I
wondered if it seemed to him strange now that for that old
woman he had left the home of his fathers, his lawful in-
heritance, and lived an exile's life.

'Have you ever been married, Captain Meadows?' I asked.

'Not me,' he said, in his shaking voice, with a grin. 'I know
too much about women for that.'

110   'That's what you say,' answered Mrs Meadows. 'If the truth
was known I shouldn't be surprised to hear that you'd had
half a dozen black wives in your day.'

'They're not black in China, Emily, you ought to know
better than that, they're yellow.'

'Perhaps that's why you've got so yellow yourself. When I
saw you, I said to myself, why, he's got jaundice.'

'I said I'd never marry anyone but you, Emily, and I never
have.'

He said this not to cause pity or in bitterness, but as a mere
120 statement of fact, as a man might say, 'I said I'd walk twenty
miles and I've done it.' There was some satisfaction in the
speech.

'Well, you might have regretted it if you had,' she answered.

I talked a little with the old man about China.

'There's no port in China that I don't know better than you
know your coat pocket. Where a ship can go I've been. I could
keep you sitting here all day long for six months and not tell
you half the things I've seen in my day.'

'Well, one thing you've not done, George, as far as I can
130 see,' said Mrs Meadows, the mocking but not unkindly smile
still in her eyes, 'and that's to make a fortune.'

'I'm not one to save money. Make it and spend it; that's my
motto. But one thing I can say for myself: if I had the chance
of going through life again I'd take it. And there aren't many
people who'll say that.'

'No, indeed,' I said.

I looked at him with admiration and respect. He was a tooth-less, crippled, penniless old man, but he had made a success of life, for he had enjoyed it. When I left him he asked me to come and see him again next day. If I was interested in China he would tell me all the stories I wanted to hear.

Next morning I thought I would go and ask if the old man would like to see me. I strolled down the magnificent avenue of elm trees and when I came to the garden saw Mrs Meadows picking flowers. I bade her good morning and she raised her-self. She had a huge armful of white flowers. I glanced at the house and I saw that the blinds were drawn: I was surprised, for Mrs Meadows liked the sunshine.

'Time enough to live in the dark when you're buried,' she always said.

'How's Captain Meadows?' I asked her.

'He always was a wild fellow,' she answered. 'When Lizzie took him a cup of tea this morning she found he was dead.'

'Dead?'

'Yes. Died in his sleep. I was just picking these flowers to put in the room. Well, I'm glad he died in that old house. It always means a lot to those Meadows to do that.'

They had had a good deal of difficulty in persuading him to go to bed. He had talked to them of all the things that had hap-pened to him in his long life. He was happy to be back in his old home. He was proud that he had walked up the drive without assistance, and he boasted that he would live for another twenty years. But fate had been kind: death had written the full-stop in the right place.

Mrs Meadows smelt the white flowers that she held in her arms.

'Well, I'm glad he came back,' she said. 'After I married Tom Meadows and George went away, the fact is I was never quite sure that I'd married the right one.'

THE AUTHOR

W. Somerset Maugham (1874–1965) was born in Paris, but his
parents were English. They died when he was ten and he was
brought up by an uncle, a clergyman who lived in the south of
England. He studied medicine in London, and later took up writing
as a career. We learn a good deal about his early life from his novel
Of Human Bondage. Two other novels by him are *Cakes and Ale*
and *The Moon and Sixpence*. He wrote many plays and had great
talent as a writer of short stories. One of the best of these is 'The
Letter', a dramatic incident in the lives of a group of English
people in Malaya.

READING NOTES

One of Maugham's favourite ways of telling a story, which he
uses here, is to tell it as though he had been concerned in it. The
teller of the story has no part in the events, but telling it in this
way helps to make it seem real.

Line 2　pens: enclosed spaces for farm animals.

8　*unexcitable:* calm, not easily excited.

9　*their only boast:* the only thing they were proud of.

14　*the prime of life:* the best years of their life.

21　*not by a long chalk:* by no means, not at all.

22　*She was twice the man her son was:* She had a much stronger
character than her son.

26　*if:* although.

28　*in a rare degree:* to an unusual extent.

29　*She was a character:* She had a remarkable personality.

33　*who ever.* Used here rather than 'who' because it is more
emphatic.

38–9　*an old ballad.* Ballads are traditional tales in verse, often telling
a simple story of the joys and sorrows of humble people.

39　*It was quite moving:* it aroused one's sympathy.

41　*courted.* See note on line 85 of 'Eveline' (p. 15).

41–2　*when she was, when she married.* Notice that the simple past
is used in these two clauses after *when*, although the main verbs
of the sentence are in the past perfect.

44　*They heard of him on the China coast:* they heard of him when
he was on the China coast.

50 *home.* In this case a hospital or institution for old sailors with no other home.

55 *Ford.* Ford car.

57 *Just fancy.* A colloquial expression used to express surprise. *fancy* means 'imagine'.

58 *my George:* my husband George.

66 *look in:* call at the house.

69 *something in common:* something that we could talk to each other about, something we were both interested in.

76 *bunched up:* crouching, very bent.

82 *he corrected:* he corrected me (because I had not given him his proper title).

86 *Mind you.* A colloquial expression used to warn listeners that the speaker is going to say something important.

91 *I call it:* in my opinion.

93 *see you out:* live longer than you.

102 *another:* another man.

105 *fathers:* ancestors.

119 *as:* just as, in the same way as.

157 *those Meadows:* the members of the Meadows family. Mrs Meadows does not consider herself a member of the family except by marriage.

163–4 *death had written the full-stop in the right place:* the old man had died at the right time.

EXERCISES

A. Answer these questions.

1. Why had Uncle George gone away to sea?

2. Why was the farmer's wife known only as 'Mrs George'?

3. ' "Captain," he corrected.' What does this remark tell you about Uncle George?

4. What was the tone of the conversation between Uncle George and Mrs Meadows?

5. 'I'm not one to make money,' said Captain Meadows, and yet he had made a success of his life. How?

6. 'I was never sure that I'd married the right one.' Do you think she had or had not? Say why you think so.

B. Find expressions in the story with the same meaning as those below:

1. without interruption
2. the best years of (their) life
3. by no means
4. everyone obeyed her
5. an old traditional song
6. (they) had both wanted to marry (her)
7. not showing proper respect
8. lived far from home
9. that's my rule of life
10. it is always important to those Meadows

C. Put the verbs in brackets in this passage in their correct form.

They (hear) of him on the China coast. For twenty years now and then he (send) them presents; then there (be) no more news of him; when Tom Meadows (die) his wife (write) and (tell) him, but (receive) no answer; and at last they (come) to the conclusion that he must be dead. But two or three days ago to their astonishment they (receive) a letter from the matron of the sailors' home at Portsmouth. It (appear) that for the last ten years George Meadows, crippled with rheumatism, (live) there, and now, (feel) that he had not much longer to live, (want) to see once more the house in which he (be) born. Albert Meadows, his great-nephew, (go) over to Portsmouth in the Ford to fetch him and he (be) to arrive that afternoon.

D. Put the -ing form (e.g. 'doing'), the simple form (e.g. 'do') or the infinitive (e.g. 'to do') of the verbs in brackets, to make these sentences correct.

1. Uncle George was (arrive) that afternoon.
2. They thought he must (be) dead.
3. He made me (stop) the car.
4. He said he wanted (walk).

5. You ought (know) better than that.
6. It was strange (look) at those two old people.
7. I could keep you (sit) here all day.
8. I shouldn't be surprised (hear) you'd half a dozen wives.
9. I wish I had the chance of (go) through life again.
10. I saw Mrs Meadows (pick) flowers in the garden.
11. They had had difficulty in (persuade) him (go) to bed.
12. I asked if the old man would like (see) me.

E. Put the correct prepositions in the spaces in this passage. The prepositions needed are: *at, by, from, in, of, on, up, with.*

She asked me to look . . . and see him. . . . the simplicity . . . a country woman who had never been further . . . her home than London, she thought that because we had both been . . . China we must have something . . . common. The whole family were sitting . . . the kitchen, . . . its stone floor, Mrs Meadows . . . her usual chair . . . the fire, and I was amused to see that she had put . . . her best silk dress. Her son and his wife sat . . . the table . . . their children. . . . the other side . . . the fireplace sat an old man, bunched . . . . a chair.

F. Put a suitable adjective in the second sentence of each pair.

1. The Meadows never got excited. They were . . .
2. Mrs Meadows looked at Uncle George with a kindly smile. Her smile was not . . .
3. Uncle George had no teeth. He had a grin on his . . . mouth.
4. He had spent all his money. He died . . .
5. Mrs Meadows sat in her usual chair. It would have been . . . for her to sit in any other chair.

G. Subjects for composition and discussion:

1. 'Mrs Meadows was twice the man her son was.' Why did people who knew the Meadows family say this?

2. The story is called 'Home'. Think of another title and give your reasons for choosing it.

3. 'A writer's duty is to describe life as it is and not as it ought to be.' How far does Maugham do this in his descriptions of Uncle George and Mrs Meadows?

5

The Reward

LORD DUNSANY

OUR talk at the Club one day was of opportunity and determination. Some said opportunity was required for success, and
millions never had it; others that only determination was
needed. And then Jorkens joined in, all for determination. If
a man was determined to get anything, and stuck to it long
enough, he got it, said Jorkens.

'Anything?' asked Terbut.

'Anything,' Jorkens replied, 'so long as he sticks to it, and
sticks to it hard enough and long enough. Anything whatever.'

Terbut disagreed.   10

'Life is like a race,' Jorkens went on, 'in which they tire
after a while and sit down, or get interested in something else
instead. The man who keeps on wins the race.'

'And suppose a man wanted to be skating champion of the
Sahara,' said Terbut, 'and couldn't afford the money to get
there.'

'He'd make the money,' said Jorkens. 'And he'd build a
skating-rink in the Sahara and organize a competition there.
He'd be skating champion all right, if he really gave all his
time to it.'   20

'Could you tell us a case like that?' asked one of us.

'As a matter of fact, I can,' said Jorkens, 'a very similar case.'

'Let's hear it,' said Terbut.

'There was a young fellow,' said Jorkens, 'to whom his
parents probably used to say the very things that we have been
saying now; and very likely he, as many young fellows do,
may have wanted to prove them wrong. I don't know: it was a

long time ago. But, whatever his motive was, he hit on a most extraordinary ambition, and stuck to it. It was nothing less than to be appointed Court acrobat.'

'What?' said Terbut.

'Acrobat,' Jorkens went on, 'to the Court of the country in which he lived.'

'What kind of country was that?' asked Terbut.

'Never mind what country it was,' said Jorkens. 'And as a matter of fact its customs weren't so silly as you suppose. They had no post of Court acrobat, and never had had. But that didn't stop young Gorgios. That was his name. He was a good athlete when he came by his wild idea at about the age of sixteen, and had won the high jump and the hurdles and the hundred yards at his school.'

'Well, there was opportunity,' argued Terbut, 'if he was born a good athlete.'

'But wait a moment,' said Jorkens. 'You don't remain an athlete all your life, and he still had to get the post created.'

'How did he do that?' asked Terbut.

'Simply by sticking to it,' said Jorkens. 'He went into politics. They all do in that country. But he went into them harder than anyone else, and never gave up his ambition. Of course he made speeches, and fine ones, on many other subjects; but all the while he stuck to his one idea. The years went by, and the day came when he had power enough to preach his ambition openly, and he told them how the glory of their country and of its ancient throne would be increased if the post of Court acrobat were created. He gave examples of other Courts and greater ones. Of course many opposed him: that is politics. Of course it took a long time: that is politics too. But as the years went by he wore down opposing arguments, till he had taught people what a lesson it would be to all the nations to have a young athlete at Court exhibiting perfect physical fitness, and how such an example would strengthen their soldiers and enable them finally to win the just rights of the nation in victorious battle against their accursed neighbours.

And so the idea caught on; and to make a very long story short, the post of Court acrobat was duly created.

'Both parents of Gorgios were by then long dead. By then, little remained to be done: he had only to stick for a few more days to that wild idea of his, and then, when the question arose of choosing an athlete to fill the newly-made post, whom could they choose but the man who had worked for it all those years? 70

'So Gorgios was appointed acrobat to the Court, and learned so late in life, what always takes time, that his parents were right after all. It only remained then to inaugurate him. And that is where I came on the scene, wandering about Europe as I used to do in those days when food used to be cheap and I was young and could easily walk long distances. I came to that country, and they were wonderfully friendly, and they let me see the great ceremony, which took place as soon after the creation of the post as Gorgios's uniform could be got ready. And very magnificent clothing it was, a tight-fitting suit of red 80 velvet, all gay with gold buttons and shining with lines of gold lace that wound and twisted about it. The great throne-room had been turned into a kind of gymnasium, with the members of the Royal House seated along a raised platform at one end, and the principal officers standing beside and behind them. Great curtains of red and gold were hung along the walls, and the high swings of acrobats hung down with gilded ropes from the ceiling, and a row of neat hurdles was arranged on the polished floor: like the ones over which Gorgios had won his race when at school. Lights glittered, a band in pale green and 90 gold played softly, and it was indeed a splendid scene. I will not describe it to you, because everything there, the uniforms and the ladies' brilliant dresses, was utterly put in the shade by the moment when the doors opened with a flood of golden light, and the old man in his brilliant uniform appeared between them for the crowning of his life's work. His white hair and the red uniform of the Court acrobat showed each other off to perfection, and his thin figure worn with age was made all the more melancholy by the tight-fitting uniform. As though

100 tired by his long patience and the work of a lifetime, he walked
slowly in his pointed shoes and leaned on a gilded stick. He
came to the hurdles that he remembered, over which once he
had won so easy a victory. As he came to the first he looked up
for a moment with a slightly sad expression towards the royal
platform, as though he asked some question with his eyes.
Whatever the question was it was at once understood: royal
smiles were directed towards him, and gentle applause broke
out from every hand, which he understood at once, and the
old bent form moved on away from the hurdle. Once he raised
110 a hand to touch the lowest of the swings that were hung from
the roof. But again the applause broke out, assuring him that
no actual activity was expected of him. And so; having made
his bows, he was led to a seat, his life's ambition achieved. It
must have taken him more than sixty years to do it, since first
he came by that strange ambition of his. But he did it. Not
many stick to a thing for so long.'

And Jorkens uttered a quiet sigh, so clearly mourning over
some lost ambition that he himself had given up, that not even
Terbut asked him what it was.

THE AUTHOR

Lord Dunsany (1878–1957) like James Joyce was an Irishman.
He has been described as one of the most charming of modern
Irish writers of stories and plays. He was educated at Eton, one of
England's most famous public schools, and at Sandhurst Military
College. He once said that 97 per cent of his time was spent in
sport and soldiering, the rest in writing. Joseph Jorkens occurs in
a series of stories as the narrator of fantastic adventures. 'The
Reward' is an example of these stories.

READING NOTES

The club, like the London tailor, is a typically English institution. Men of similar education and interests go to their clubs to dine
and meet each other socially. The club is an excellent place for
story-telling. H. G. Wells uses it in 'The Truth about Pyecraft'
(p. 156).

Line 4. *all for:* completely in favour of.

5 *stuck to it:* persisted.

8 *so long as:* provided that, on condition that.

11 *they:* i.e. 'the runners'.

14–15 *skating champion of the Sahara.* Terbut chooses the most impossible thing he can think of.

18 *skating-rink:* a place made for skating.

19 *all right.* A conversational phrase which emphasises the speaker's belief in what he is saying. 'He'd certainly be skating champion'.

26 *very likely:* probably.

28 *hit on:* chose, thought of.

35 *Never mind:* it doesn't matter.

39 *came by:* the same meaning as *hit on. Come by* can also mean 'acquire', e.g. How did you come by that valuable picture?
Notice also 'come across', which means 'find' or 'meet unexpectedly', e.g. When I was looking at some old books in a bookshop, I came across an interesting travel book about Brazil.

40 *hurdles.* A race in which the runners have to jump over a number of wooden hurdles or fences as they run.

40–1 *the hundred yards:* the hundred-yards race.

48 *them:* i.e. 'politics'.

51 *all the while:* all the time.

56 *many:* many people.

62–3 *just rights, accursed neighbours.* The writer is making fun of political propaganda. One's own country is always right, and its enemies are always wrong.

64 *caught on:* was accepted, became popular.

65 *duly:* as a result of Gorgios's efforts.

70 *but:* except.

72 *what always takes time.* This refers to the learning of the lesson.

73 *after all:* i.e. contrary to what he had believed.
inaugurate him: appoint him officially.

74 *came on the scene:* arrived at the place where this was happening.

77 *they:* i.e. the people of the country.

82 *wound.* Pronounced [waund], the past tense of 'wind' (pronounced [waind]), meaning 'move in curves'. We speak of a river winding through the fields in a valley.

87 *swings.* A swing is a seat suspended from ropes, on which children or acrobats move forwards and backwards.

90–1 *in pale green and gold:* in pale green uniforms with gold lace on them.

93 *was put in the shade:* seemed less brilliant by comparison.

96 *the crowning:* the supreme moment, the reward.

97 *showed each other off:* contrasted with each other and therefore emphasised each other.

103 *the first:* the first hurdle.

108 *from every hand:* from every side. In this case hands may be referred to literally, since the people clapped their hands; but *hand* is also used to mean 'side' when hands literally are not involved, e.g. in the expressions 'on the one hand', 'on the other hand', used to put opposite sides of an argument.

113 *achieved:* having been achieved.

118 *some ambition:* an ambition not known or explained.

EXERCISES

A. Answer these questions.

    1. What was the subject discussed at the club?

    2. What did Terbut think of Jorkens's argument?

    3. How did Jorkens suggest that a man could become skating champion of the Sahara?

    4. Does the story give any idea of Jorkens's political views? if so, what were they?

    5. How did Gorgios achieve his ambition?

    6. Why were the brilliant dresses put in the shade at the inauguration?

    7. 'Gentle applause broke out.' Why was the applause gentle?

    8. Were Gorgios's parents proved right?

B. Complete each sentence to agree with the story by choosing the most suitable of the phrases in brackets.

    1. Jorkens said that a man who wanted to succeed had to be (an athlete, a determined person, a lucky man).

2. Gorgios probably wanted to (make his country powerful, prove his parents wrong, wear a splendid uniform).
3. When Gorgios was inaugurated, the people applauded because he (had achieved his ambition, looked splendid in his uniform, performed on the hurdles and swings).
4. Terbut (asked Jorkens what his own ambition was, believed Jorkens's story, disagreed with Jorkens's opinion).
5. Gorgios achieved his ambition by (building a skating-rink, going into politics, winning the hundred yards).

C. Complete these sentences with the correct past forms of the verbs in brackets.

1. Jorkens said that if a man (be) determined to get anything, and (stick) to it long enough, he (get) it.
2. If a man (want) to be skating champion of the Sahara, and (can) not afford the money to get there, he (make) the money.
3. He (be) skating champion if he (give) all his time to it.
4. It was thought that the glory of the country (be) increased if the post of Court acrobat (be) created.
5. It was decided that if a good athlete (can) be found, they (make) him Court acrobat.

D. Find expressions in the story with the same meaning as those below:

1. determination was the one essential
2. he could not pay
3. he picked an aim in life
4. he became a politician
5. he persisted in (his idea)
6. (The years) passed
7. he made (them) agree with him
8. the idea became popular
9. everything was outshone by
10. each made the other look perfect

E. Rewrite the sentences below, using the correct form of one of these expressions: *come across, come back, come by, come in, come over.*

1. Papa returned home from London after his day's work.
2. Frank had travelled from Buenos Aires to Dublin to marry Eveline.
3. Jorkens didn't know how Gorgios had thought of the idea of becoming Court acrobat.
4. When the doors opened, Gorgios entered, wearing a brilliant uniform.
5. I sometimes find a cheap suit at the Sales.

F. Complete these sentences.

1. If you stick . . . a thing long enough, you'll get it.
2. Some runners tire . . . a while.
3. Gorgios hit . . . an extraordinary ambition.
4. Jorkens was all . . . determination.
5. He went . . . politics.
6. The years went . . .
7. The question arose . . . choosing a court acrobat.
8. That is where I came . . . the scene.
9. The throne-room had been turned . . . a gymnasium.
10. He remembered the hurdles . . . which he had won an easy victory.

G. Subjects for composition and discussion:

1. Imagine you are Gorgios, and make a short political speech in favour of having a Court acrobat.
2. Make a speech in reply to Gorgios, opposing his proposal.
3. ' "The Reward" is an amusing story with a serious side to it.' Discuss this.
4. 'The man who keeps on wins the race.' 'Opportunity is required for success.' Does the story prove either of these statements?

6

The Singing Lesson

KATHERINE MANSFIELD

WITH DESPAIR – cold, sharp despair – buried deep in her heart like a wicked knife, Miss Meadows, in cap and gown and carrying a little baton, trod the cold corridors that led to the music hall. Girls of all ages, rosy from the air, and bubbling over with that gleeful excitement that comes from running to school on a fine autumn morning, hurried, skipped, fluttered by; from the hollow classrooms came a quick drumming of voices; a bell rang; a voice like a bird cried, 'Muriel.' And then there came from the staircase a tremendous knock-knock-knocking. Someone had dropped her dumbbells.

The Science Mistress stopped Miss Meadows.

'Good mor-ning,' she cried, in her sweet, affected drawl. 'Isn't it cold? It might be win-ter.'

Miss Meadows, hugging the knife, stared in hatred at the Science Mistress. Everything about her was sweet, pale, like honey. You would not have been surprised to see a bee caught in the tangles of that yellow hair.

'It is rather sharp,' said Miss Meadows, grimly.

The other smiled her sugary smile.

'You look fro-zen,' said she. Her blue eyes opened wide; there came a mocking light in them. (Had she noticed anything?)

'Oh, not quite as bad as that,' said Miss Meadows, and she gave the Science Mistress, in exchange for her smile, a quick grimace and passed on . . .

Forms Four, Five and Six were assembled in the music hall. The noise was deafening. On the platform, by the piano, stood

Mary Beazley, Miss Meadows' favourite, who played accompaniments. She was turning the music stool. When she saw Miss Meadows she gave a loud, warning 'Sh-sh! girls!' and Miss Meadows, her hands thrust in her sleeves, the baton under her arm, strode down the centre aisle, mounted the steps, urned sharply, seized the brass music stand, planted it in front of her, and gave two sharp taps with her baton for silence.

'Silence, please! Immediately!' and, looking at nobody, her glance swept over that sea of coloured flannel blouses, with bobbing pink faces and hands, quivering butterfly hair-bows, and music-books outspread. She knew perfectly well what they were thinking. 'Meady is in a wax.' Well, let them think it! Her eyelids quivered; she tossed her head, defying them. What could the thoughts of those creatures matter to someone who stood there bleeding to death, pierced to the heart, to the heart, by such a letter —

'. . . I feel more and more strongly that our marriage would be a mistake. Not that I do not love you. I love you as much as it is possible for me to love any woman, but, truth to tell, I have come to the conclusion that I am not a marrying man, and the idea of settling down fills me with nothing but —' and the word 'disgust' was scratched out lightly and 'regret' written over the top.

Basil! Miss Meadows stalked over to the piano. And Mary Beazley, who was waiting for this moment, bent forward; her curls fell over her cheeks while she breathed, 'Good morning, Miss Meadows.' and she motioned towards rather than handed to her mistress a beautiful yellow chrysanthemum. This little ritual of the flower had been gone through for ages and ages, quite a term and a half. It was as much part of the lesson as opening the piano. But this morning, instead of taking it up, instead of tucking it into her belt while she leant over Mary and said 'Thank you, Mary. How very nice! Turn to page thirty-two,' what was Mary's horror when Miss Meadows totally ignored the chrysanthemum, made no reply to her greeting, but said in a voice of ice, 'Page fourteen, please, and mark the accents well.'

Staggering moment! Mary blushed until the tears stood in her eyes, but Miss Meadows had gone back to the music stand; her voice rang through the music hall.

'Page fourteen. We will begin with page fourteen. "A Lament." Now, girls, you ought to know it by this time. We shall take it all together; not in parts, all together. And without expression. Sing it through quite simply, beating time with the left hand.'

She raised the baton; she tapped the music stand twice. Down came Mary on the opening chord; down came all those left hands, beating the air, and in chimed those young, mournful voices:

> Fast! Ah, too fast fade the roses of pleasure;
> Soon Autumn yields unto Wi-i-nter drear.
> Fleetly! Ah, fleetly mu-u-sic's gay measure
> Passes away from the listening ear.

Good heavens, what could be more tragic than that lament! Every note was a sigh, a sob, a groan of awful mournfulness. Miss Meadows lifted her arms in the wide gown and began conducting with both hands '. . . I feel more and more strongly that our marriage would be a mistake . . .' she beat. And the voices cried: *Fleetly! Ah, fleetly.* What could have possessed him to write such a letter? What could have led up to it? It came out of nothing. His last letter had been all about a fumed oak bookcase he had bought for 'our' books, and a 'natty little hallstand' he had seen, 'a very neat affair with a carved owl on a bracket, holding three hat-brushes in its claws'. How she had smiled at that! So like a man to think one needed three hat-brushes! *From the listening ear*, sang the voices.

'Once again,' said Miss Meadows. 'But this time in parts. Still without expression.' *Fast! Ah, too fast.* With the gloom of the contraltos added, one could scarcely help shuddering. *Fade the roses of pleasure.* Last time he had come to see her, Basil

had worn a rose in his buttonhole. How handsome he had
looked in that bright blue suit, with that dark red rose! And
he knew it, too. He couldn't help knowing it. First he stroked
his hair, then his moustache; his teeth gleamed when he
smiled . . .

'The headmaster's wife keeps on asking me to dinner. It's
a perfect nuisance. I never get an evening to myself in that
place.'

'But can't you refuse?'

'Oh, well, it doesn't do for a man in my position to be un-
popular.'

Music's gay measure, wailed the voices. The willow trees,
outside the high, narrow windows, waved in the wind. They
had lost half their leaves. The tiny ones that clung wriggled
like fishes caught on a line. '. . . I am not a marrying man . . .'
The voices were silent; the piano waited.

'Quite good,' said Miss Meadows, but still in such a strange,
stony tone that the younger girls began to feel positively
frightened. 'But now that we know it, we shall take it with
expression. As much expression as you can put into it. Think
of the words, girls. Use your imaginations. *Fast! Ah, too fast*,'
cried Miss Meadows. 'That ought to break out – a loud, strong
forte – a lament. And then in the second line, *Winter drear*,
make that *drear* sound as if a cold wind were blowing through
it. *Dre-ear!*' said she so awfully that Mary Beazley, on the
music stool, wriggled her spine. 'The third line should be one
crescendo. *Fleetly! Ah, fleetly music's gay measure*. Breaking
on the first word of the last line, *Passes*. And then on the word,
away, you must begin to die . . . to fade . . . until *the listening
ear* is nothing more than a faint whisper . . . You can slow
down as much as you like almost on the last line. Now,
please.'

Again the two light taps; she lifted her arms again. *Fast!
Ah, too fast*. '. . . and the idea of settling down fills me with
nothing but disgust –' Disgust was what he had written. That
was as good as to say their engagement was definitely broken

off. Broken off! Their engagement! People had been surprised enough that she had got engaged. The Science Mistress would not believe it at first. But nobody had been as surprised as she. She was thirty. Basil was twenty-five. It had been a miracle, simply a miracle, to hear him say, as they walked home from church that very dark night, 'You know, somehow or other, 140 I've got fond of you.' And he had taken hold of the end of her ostrich feather boa. *Passes away from the listening ear*.

'Repeat! Repeat!' said Miss Meadows. 'More expression, girls! Once more!'

Fast! Ah, too fast. The older girls were crimson; some of the younger ones began to cry. Big spots of rain blew against the windows, and one could hear the willows whispering, '. . . not that I do not love you . . .'

'But, my darling, if you love me,' thought Miss Meadows, 'I don't mind how much it is. Love me as little as you like.' 150 But she knew he didn't love her. Not to have cared enough to scratch out that 'disgust', so that she couldn't read it! *Soon Autumn yields unto Winter drear*. She would have to leave the school, too. She could never face the Science Mistress or the girls after it got known. She would have to disappear some-where. *Passes away*. The voices began to die, to fade, to whisper . . . to vanish . . .

Suddenly the door opened. A little girl in blue walked fussily up the aisle, hanging her head, biting her lips, and twisting the silver bangle on her red little wrist. She came up 160 the steps and stood before Miss Meadows.

'Well, Monica, what is it?'

'Oh, if you please, Miss Meadows,' said the little girl, gasping, 'Miss Wyatt wants to see you in the mistresses' room.'

'Very well,' said Miss Meadows. And she called to the girls, 'I shall put you on your honour to talk quietly while I am away.' But they were too subdued to do anything else. Most of them were blowing their noses.

The corridors were silent and cold; they echoed to Miss Meadows' steps. The head mistress sat at her desk. For a 170 moment she did not look up. She was as usual disentangling her eyeglasses, which had got caught in her lace tie. 'Sit down, Miss Meadows,' she said very kindly. And then she picked up a pink envelope from the blotting-pad. 'I sent for you just now because this telegram has come for you.'

'A telegram for me, Miss Wyatt?'

Basil! He had committed suicide, decided Miss Meadows. Her hand flew out, but Miss Wyatt held the telegram back a moment. 'I hope it's not bad news,' she said, no more than 180 kindly. And Miss Meadows tore it open.

'Pay no attention to letter must have been mad bought hat-stand today Basil,' she read. She couldn't take her eyes off the telegram.

'I do hope it's nothing very serious,' said Miss Wyatt, leaning forward.

'Oh, no, thank you, Miss Wyatt,' blushed Miss Meadows. 'It's nothing bad at all. It's' – and she gave an apologetic little laugh – 'it's from my *fiancé* saying that . . . saying that –' There was a pause. 'I *see*,' said Miss Wyatt. And another pause. 190 Then – 'You've fifteen minutes more of your class, Miss Meadows, haven't you?'

'Yes, Miss Wyatt.' She got up. She half ran towards the door.

'Oh, just one minute, Miss Meadows,' said Miss Wyatt. 'I must say I don't approve of my teachers having telegrams sent to them in school hours, unless in case of very bad news, such as death,' explained Miss Wyatt, 'or a very serious accident or something to that effect. Good news, Miss Meadows, will always keep, you know.'

200 On the wings of hope, of love, of joy, Miss Meadows sped back to the music hall, up the aisle, up the steps, over to the piano.

'Page thirty-two, Mary,' she said, 'page thirty-two,' and picking up the yellow chrysanthemum she held it to her lips to hide her smile. Then she turned to the girls, rapped with her baton: 'Page thirty-two, girls. Page thirty-two.'

We come here today with flowers o'erladen,
With baskets of fruit and ribbons to boot,
To-oo congratulate . . .

'Stop! Stop!' cried Miss Meadows. 'This is awful. This is 210 dreadful.' And she beamed at her girls. 'What's the matter with you all? Think, girls, think of what you're singing. Use your imaginations. *With flowers o'erladen. Baskets of fruit and ribbons to boot.* And *congratulate*,' Miss Meadows broke off. 'Don't look so doleful, girls. It ought to sound warm, joyful, eager. *Congratulate*. Once more. Quickly. All together. Now then!'

And this time Miss Meadows' voice sounded over all the other voices – full, deep, glowing with expression.

THE AUTHOR

Katherine Mansfield (1883–1923) was born in New Zealand. She came to England to finish her education and married J. Middleton Murry, a well-known writer on literary topics. She died in France after a long illness. Although her life was short, she soon became well known, both in Britain and on the Continent of Europe, for her short stories. Her special qualities are, in the words of one critic, 'her tender humanity, her clarity, her wit, and her courageous gaiety'. 'The Singing Lesson' comes from a collection of short stories which takes its title from the first story in the collection, 'The Garden Party'. Readers who like 'The Singing Lesson' would certainly enjoy 'The Garden Party', which is perhaps her best-known story.

READING NOTES

'The Singing Lesson' is a psychological study. The way in which a music teacher shows her emotions through the songs that she teaches her class is cleverly worked out.

Line 2 cap and gown. The academic costume which teachers wear in some secondary schools.
3 *trod:* walked along (present tense, *tread*).

7 *drumming.* The voices in the classrooms sounded like drums being beaten.

10 *dumbbells.* These are bars with a round weight on each end which are used in gymnasiums. They made this repeated knocking sound as they rolled down the staircase.

12 The hyphens here and in lines 13 and 20 represent the Science Mistress's drawl.

14 *the knife.* Lines 2 and 45–51 explain this.

26 *Forms Four, Five and Six.* In secondary schools the classes are called *Forms.* They number up from One to Six, the youngest pupils being in Form One and the oldest in Form Six. (In primary schools the classes are called 'Class'.)

31 *her sleeves:* the long, wide sleeves of her gown.

36 *looking at nobody:* i.e. at no individual girl.

38 *hair-bows. Bows* in this case, meaning ribbons tied in a knot with loops, is pronounced [bouz].

40 *in a wax.* Schoolgirls' slang for 'in a bad temper', 'angry'.

47 *truth to tell:* to tell the truth.

48 *a marrying man:* the kind of man who wants to get married.

49 *settling down:* leading a quiet, regular life.

52 *stalked:* walked in a stiff manner which showed that she was angry.

57 *ages and ages.* Another example of schoolgirls' slang, in this case an exaggeration, as the rest of the sentence shows.

58 *term.* The school year in Britain is divided into three sessions called 'terms', with a holiday after each.

60 *tucking.* This suggests 'pushing something into a small space'.

63 *totally ignored:* took no notice at all of.

65 *accents:* marks in the music showing how it should be played.

66 *staggering:* astonishing (because such strong emotion makes one's legs feel weak).

70 *Lament:* a sad song.

71 *not in parts.* To sing in parts means that several voices sing different tunes at the same time, in harmony. The opposite, when all voices sing the same tune, is to sing in unison.

72 *beating time:* moving one's hand to mark the rhythm of the music. The beat is the time given by the conductor, who beats time by the movements of his baton or his hand.

79 *drear.* Poetic form of 'dreary'.

80 *fleetly*. A poetic word meaning 'quickly'.

87–8 *What could have possessed him:* What madness had seized him.

88–9 *It came out of nothing:* There was no reason for it.

90 *natty*. A colloquial word for 'smart'.

96 *gloom:* sadness, mournful sound.

97 *help:* avoid.

104 *the headmaster's wife*. Basil is evidently a schoolmaster.

108 *It doesn't do:* It isn't wise, It isn't a good thing.

110 *wailed:* sang sadly.

112 *ones:* i.e. leaves.

124–5 *one crescendo:* a single, continuous crescendo.

125 *Breaking:* Making a pause.

134 *as good as to say:* just like saying.

134–5 *broken off:* ended.

142 *boa*. A scarf made of feathers, which ladies used to wear round their necks.

146–7 *spots of rain, willows whispering*. The weather and the trees seem to be sad, in harmony with Miss Meadows' present mood.

151 *cared:* loved her.

154 *face:* meet. *Face* as a verb generally suggests meeting something unpleasant.

159 *fussily*. The meaning of this word depends on the context in which it is used. Here it suggests that the little girl was behaving in a self-conscious way, feeling important as she interrupted the big girls' lesson.

164 *the mistresses' room:* the teachers' room.

172 *her lace tie:* i.e. piece of lace worn round her neck.

173 *very kindly*. The headmistress spoke kindly because she had a telegram for Miss Meadows. Many people send telegrams only to announce urgent news of illness or death.

179–80 *no more than kindly*. The headmistress was perhaps a little annoyed at Miss Meadows' eagerness to take the telegram from her.

200 *sped:* went quickly (from 'speed'). A literary word.

201 *over:* across the platform.

203 *Page thirty-two*. The song the girls had expected to sing was on this page. (See lines 61–2.) The reasons why Miss Meadows had chosen the lament at first and now turns to this song are obvious.

205 *rapped:* struck the music stand sharply with her baton.

207 *with flowers o'erladen:* loaded with great quantities of flowers.
O'erladen [ɔːleidn] is a poetic form of 'overladen'.

208 *to boot:* as well, in addition. An old-fashioned expression.

215 *doleful:* mournful, sad.

216–17 *Now then.* A good example of an idiomatic colloquial
phrase. The two words separately have opposite meanings. Used
together, they form a lively way of saying 'Are you ready?' or
'Let's begin'.

EXERCISES

A. Answer these questions.

  1. Why didn't Miss Meadows like the Science Mistress?
  2. 'Had she noticed anything?' What might the Science
     Mistress have noticed?
  3. How did Miss Meadows behave when Mary Beazley
     offered her the chrysanthemum?
  4. How did Mary expect her to behave?
  5. What was the effect of her behaviour on the girls?
  6. What kind of man do you think Basil was? Give reasons
     for your answer.
  7. Why did the headmistress stop speaking kindly to Miss
     Meadows?
  8. How did Miss Meadows show her change of feelings
     after she had read the telegram?

B. Find expressions in the story with the same meaning as
those below.

  1. with pink cheeks [from the fresh air outside]
  2. looked fixedly and with dislike
  3. she looked from side to side of the class
  4. getting married and setting up house
  5. (She) walked stiffly
  6. What strange motive had he for writing?
  7. as if he had said
  8. they were no longer engaged
  9. (I) behaved as if I were mad

10. Good news is never
    urgent

C. Use the most suitable of these expressions in a proper position in each of the sentences below, instead of the words in italics: *awfully, definitely, fussily, grimly, lightly, more and more strongly, perfectly well, positively, quietly, sharply*.

1. Miss Meadows turned *with a sudden movement*.
2. She knew *exactly* what they were thinking.
3. I feel *more certain as time goes on* that our marriage would be a mistake.
4. The young girls began to feel *really* frightened.
5. A little girl in blue walked up the aisle *in an awkward manner*.
6. 'It is rather sharp,' said Miss Meadows *in a severe voice*.
7. The word 'disgust' was scratched out, *but not heavily enough*.
8. 'Dre-ear!' said she *in a frightening voice*.
9. The engagement was broken off *without any doubt*.
10. I shall put you on your honour to talk while I am away *without making a lot of noise*.

D. Complete these sentences with suitable prepositions or adverbs.

1. Their voices bubbled . . . excitement.
2. Girls of all ages hurried . . .
3. The idea . . . settling down fills me . . . disgust.
4. The word 'disgust' was scratched . . .
5. Instead . . . taking . . . the flower, she ignored it.
6. It came out . . . nothing.
7. What could have led . . . to it?
8. You can slow . . . as much as you like on the last line.
9. . . . came Mary's hands on the opening chord.
10. Her hand flew . . . to take the telegram.

E. Imagine that the fussy little girl in blue had listened to the following conversation and that she is telling someone else what she heard. Begin with 'Miss Wyatt asked . . .' and use *asked*, *said* and *answered* where they are needed.

Please sit down, Miss Meadows. I sent for you because a telegram has come for you.

You have a telegram for me, Miss Wyatt?

Yes, I have. I hope it's not bad news. I do hope it's nothing very serious.

It isn't anything serious. It's nothing bad at all. It's from my fiancé.

I don't approve of my teachers having telegrams sent to them in school hours, unless there is bad news. Good news will keep.

F.   Subjects for composition and discussion:
  1. 'Miss Meadows and Basil would probably be unhappy if they married.' Say whether you think the story suggests this. Give reasons for your opinion.
  2. Which of the writer's qualities of 'tender humanity, clarity, wit and courageous gaiety' are shown in this story?
  5. The effect of the story depends a good deal on contrasts. Mention what contrasts you have noticed in it.

7

The Open Window

SAKI

'MY aunt will be down presently, Mr Nuttel,' said a very self-possessed young lady of fifteen; 'in the meantime you must try and put up with me.'

Framton Nuttel tried to say a few words which should flatter both the niece of the moment and the aunt that was to come. Privately he doubted more than ever whether these formal visits on a number of total strangers would do much towards helping the nerve cure which he was to undergo.

'I know how it will be,' his sister had said when he was preparing to leave for the country; 'you will bury yourself down 10 there and not speak to anybody, and your nerves will be worse than ever from moping. I shall just give you letters of introduction to all the people I know there. Some of them, as far as I can remember, were quite nice.'

Framton wondered whether Mrs Sappleton, the lady to whom he was presenting one of the letters of introduction, was one of the nice people.

'Do you know many of the people round here?' asked the niece, when she thought that they had been silent long enough. 20

'Hardly anybody,' said Framton. 'My sister was staying here, at the rectory, you know, some four years ago, and she gave me letters of introduction to some of the people here.'

He said the last sentence in a tone that showed his regret.

'Then you know practically nothing about my aunt?' continued the self-possessed young lady.

'Only her name and address,' admitted the visitor. He was

wondering whether Mrs Sappleton was in the married or
widowed state. Something about the room made him believe
30 the former.

'Her great tragedy happened just three years ago,' said the
child; 'that would be since your sister's time.'

'Her tragedy?' asked Framton; somehow in this restful
country spot tragedies seemed out of place.

'You may wonder why we keep that window wide open on
an October afternoon,' said the niece, pointing out a large
French window that opened on to a lawn.

'It is quite warm for the time of the year,' said Framton;
'but has that window got anything to do with her tragedy?'

40 'Out through that window, three years ago to a day, her
husband and her two young brothers went off for their day's
shooting. They never came back. In crossing the moor to their
favourite snipe-shooting ground they were all three engulfed
in a treacherous part of the marsh. It had been that dreadful
wet summer, you know, and places that were safe in other
years gave way suddenly without warning. Their bodies were
never recovered. That was the dreadful part of it.' Here the
child's voice lost its self-possessed note and became hesitatingly
human. 'Poor aunt always thinks that they will come back
50 some day, they and the little brown spaniel that was lost with
them, and walk in at that window just as they used to do. That
is why the window is kept open every evening until it is quite
dusk. Poor dear aunt, she has often told me how they went out,
her husband with his white raincoat over his arm, and Ronnie,
her youngest brother, singing "Bertie, why do you bound?"
as he always did to tease her, because she said it got on her
nerves. Do you know, sometimes on still, quiet evenings like
this, I almost get a creepy feeling that they will all walk in
through that window – '

60 She broke off with a little shudder. It was a relief to Framton when the aunt hurried into the room with many apologies
for being late.

'I hope Vera has been amusing you?' she said.

'She has been very interesting,' said Framton.

'I hope you don't mind the open window,' said Mrs Sappleton, 'my husband and brothers will be home directly from shooting, and they always come in this way. They've been out for snipe in the marshes today, so they'll make a fine mess over my poor carpets. So like you men-folk, isn't it?'

She rattled on cheerfully about the shooting and the scarcity of birds, and the prospects for duck in the winter. To Framton it was all purely horrible. He made a desperate effort to turn the talk to a less horrible subject; but he was conscious that his hostess was giving him only a small part of her attention, and her eyes were constantly wandering past him to the open window and the lawn beyond. It was certainly an unfortunate coincidence that he should have paid his visit on this tragic anniversary.

'The doctors agree in ordering me complete rest, as well as avoidance of mental excitement and violent physical exercise,' announced Framton, who, like many people, mistakenly believed that total strangers and chance acquaintances are hungry for every detail of one's illnesses, their cause and cure. 'On the matter of diet they are not so much in agreement,' he continued.

'No?' said Mrs Sappleton, in a voice which only replaced a yawn at the last moment. Then she suddenly brightened into alert attention – but not to what Framton was saying.

'Here they are at last!' she cried. 'Just in time for tea, and don't they look as if they were muddy up to the eyes!'

Framton shivered slightly and turned towards the niece with a look intended to show sympathetic understanding. The child was staring out through the open window with dazed horror in her eyes. In a cold shock of nameless fear Framton swung round in his seat and looked in the same direction.

In the deepening twilight three figures were walking across the lawn towards the window; they all carried guns under their arms, and one of them was burdened with a white coat hung over his shoulders. A tired brown spaniel kept close at

100 their heels. Noiselessly they neared the house, and then a hoarse young voice sang out of the dusk: 'I said, Bertie, why do you bound?'

Framton grabbed wildly at his stick and hat; the hall-door, the gravel drive, and the front gate were dimly noted stages in his hasty retreat. A cyclist coming along the road had to run into the hedge to avoid colliding with him.

'Here we are, my dear,' said the bearer of the white rain-coat, coming in through the window; 'fairly muddy, but most of it's dry. Who was that who rushed out as we came up?'

110 'A most extraordinary man, a Mr Nuttel,' said Mrs Sapple-ton; 'could only talk about his illnesses, and rushed off without a word of good-bye or apology when you arrived. One would think he had seen a ghost.'

'I expect it was the spaniel,' said the niece calmly; 'he told me he had a horror of dogs. He was once hunted into a ceme-tery somewhere on the banks of the Ganges by a pack of wild dogs, and had to spend the night in a newly dug grave with the creatures snarling and grinning and foaming just above him. Enough to make anyone lose their nerve.'

120 Romance at short notice was her speciality.

THE AUTHOR

'Saki' was the pen-name of Hector Hugh Munro (1870–1916). He began his literary career as a political journalist. In this pro-fession he worked in Russia and France. He published several volumes of short stories, the best-known being *The Chronicles of Clovis*. He lost his life while serving as a soldier in the 1914–18 war. His stories show an understanding of children and of young people who play cleverly and sometimes maliciously on the feelings of their elders. He also shows a sympathetic understanding of animals, which play major roles in some of his other stories.

READING NOTES

This story, like 'The Awful Fate of Melpomenus Jones' by Stephen Leacock, makes fun of the dislike that people are supposed to feel for making and receiving social calls. It also presents one of the most malicious of his young people.

Line 1 *will be down presently:* will come down soon.

2–3 *try and put up with:* try to be content with, try to endure.

5 *the niece of the moment:* the niece who was entertaining him at the moment.

6 *more than ever.* He had already been thinking that these visits would be bad for him. Now he was even more certain.

7 *total strangers:* people he had never met and about whom he knew nothing.

10 *bury yourself:* hide away from people.

12 *moping:* living alone and feeling miserable.

22 *rectory:* the house of the rector or parish priest.

25 *practically nothing:* hardly anything.

32 *your sister's time:* the time when your sister was here.

34 *out of place:* unlikely, unsuitable to the surroundings.

37 *French window.* A glass door opening on to the garden.

38 *warm for the time of year:* i.e. you would not expect it to be so warm at this time of year.

40 *to a day:* exactly.

42 *moor:* wild, uncultivated land.

44 *treacherous.* Because the green grass made the surface look firm.

46 *gave way:* collapsed.

48–9 *hesitatingly human.* The girl's voice broke off, as if she were overcome by her human feeling of pity for her aunt.

55 *Bertie, why do you bound?* A popular song of the early twentieth century. *Bound* means 'jump', but here there is a play on words, because 'bounder' means a person whose behaviour is unpleasant to other people.

58 *creepy.* A word used by children, meaning 'frightening' (as if something unpleasant were creeping up one's back).

63 *I hope Vera has been amusing you.* An example of Saki's irony.

66 *directly:* immediately.

68 *a fine mess:* a sarcastic expression for a 'lot of dirt'. Compare with 'You're a fine one', said to someone who has caused a lot of trouble.

70 *rattled on:* went on talking rapidly.

71 *duck.* Hunters speak of ducks collectively in this way. (*Snipe* always has the same form in the singular and plural.)

87 *she suddenly brightened.* Mrs Sappleton had been bored by Frampton's description of his illness, but she grew cheerful as she saw the shooting-party approaching.

104 *drive.* A private road leading to a house.

116 *the banks of the Ganges.* Vera chose a river in India to make her story more romantic, and also to make the 'pack of wild dogs' more easily believed.

118 *foaming.* Mad dogs have foam at their mouths.

119 *their.* Used in conversation, after expressions such as 'anyone', 'everyone', 'nobody', to avoid the clumsy though correct expression 'his or her'.

120 *at short notice:* with little time for preparation.

EXERCISES

A. Answer these questions.

   1. What did you learn from the first two paragraphs of the story about the people in it?

   2. What tragedy did Vera describe?

   3. Why was Mrs Sappleton's conversation horrible to Mr Nuttel?

   4. At what moment did Mr Nuttel make his escape?

   5. 'One would think he had seen a ghost.' Why did he act as if he had seen one?

   6. What was Vera's explanation of the visitor's strange behaviour?

   7. 'Romance at short notice was her speciality.' How does the story show this?

   8. Do you think Mr Nuttel deserved to be treated like this? If so, why?

B. Choose the correct one of these expressions to complete each of the sentences below: *dazed, diet, dusk, for the time of year, on my nerves, out of place, self-possessed, since her time, without a word of apology, without warning.*

   1. The child was not shy of strangers. She was perfectly . . .

   2. Tragedies seemed . . . in this peaceful country spot.

 3. Your sister does not know about the tragedy, it happened . . .

  4. They will stay out shooting till it is . . .

  5. The visitor rushed away . . .

  6. The treacherous marsh gave way . . .

  7. It is unusually warm . . .

  8. People who tell me about their illnesses get . . .

  9. My sister is too fat. The doctor has ordered her a strict . . .

  10. The cyclist was . . . by the collision.

C. Give the correct form of the verbs in brackets.

  1. He doubted whether these formal visits would do much towards (help) the nerve cure.

  2. Your nerves will be worse than ever from (mope).

  3. You must try and (put up) with me.

  4. A cyclist was obliged (run) into the hedge to avoid (collide) with him.

  5. He was preparing (leave) for the country.

  6. The dogs spent the night (snarl) above the grave.

  7. She left the window open for the men (come) in from shooting.

  8. He regretted (have) letters of introduction to his sister's acquaintances.

  9. You may wonder at our (keep) the window open in October.

  10. In (cross) the moor for a day's shooting they were lost for ever.

D. Put the expressions in brackets in the most suitable place in these sentences.

  1. 'My aunt will be down,' said Vera. (presently)

  2. He doubted more than ever if these visits would do him any good. (privately)

  3. I shall give you letters of introduction to all the people I know. (just, there)

4. My sister was staying at the rectory some four years ago. (here)
5. 'Then you know nothing about my aunt?' continued the young lady. (practically)
6. Places that were safe in other years gave way. (without warning, suddenly)
7. The child's voice became human. (hesitatingly)
8. Poor dear aunt, she has told me how they went out. (often)
9. She rattled on about the shooting. (cheerfully)
10. Framton shivered as she greeted her husband. (slightly)

E. Rewrite the sentences below using adjectives from the story instead of the phrases in brackets.

Example
The niece was a young lady (with a calm and assured manner).
The niece was a self-possessed young lady.

1. This winter snipe and duck are (difficult to find because there are not many of them).
2. He paid a number of visits (merely out of a sense of duty).
3. I do not like discussing my private affairs with acquaintances (whom I have met accidentally).
4. The niece thought they had been long enough (without speaking to each other).
5. He introduced me to his brother (that he liked best).
6. It is a quiet evening. Even the birds are (not moving or singing).
7. They walked over the carpet with their boots (covered with earth).
8. In the twilight (which grew darker every moment) he could distinguish the older man's white raincoat.
9. The shooting party returned with a brown spaniel (which wanted to lie down and rest).

10. The singer could not perform at the concert because a cold had left her (with a weak and unmusical voice).

F. Imagine you are Mrs Sappleton on a visit to the rector's wife. Tell the rector's wife what Mr Nuttel said to you and how he behaved.

G. Subjects for composition and discussion:

1. A conversation between two doctors about Mr Nuttel.
2. Mrs Sappleton's niece was a naughty girl and ought to have been punished.

   Mrs Sappleton's niece was a clever girl and was quite right to do what she did.

   Which of these opinions do you agree with? Give reasons for your answer.

8

How to Grow Old

BERTRAND RUSSELL

IN spite of the title, this article will really be on how *not* to grow old, which, at my time of life, is a much more important subject. My first advice would be to choose your ancestors carefully. Although both my parents died young, I have done well in this respect as regards my other ancestors. My maternal grandfather, it is true, was cut off in the flower of his youth at the age of sixty-seven, but my other three grandparents all lived to be over eighty. Of remoter ancestors I can only discover one who did not live to a great age, and he died of a
10 disease which is now rare, namely, having his head cut off. A great-grandmother of mine, who was a friend of Gibbon, lived to the age of ninety-two, and to her last day remained a terror to all her descendants. My maternal grandmother, after having nine children who survived, one who died in infancy, and many miscarriages, as soon as she became a widow devoted herself to women's higher education. She was one of the founders of Girton College, and worked hard at opening the medical profession to women. She used to tell of how she met in Italy an elderly gentleman who was looking very sad. She
20 asked him why he was so melancholy and he said that he had just parted from his two grandchildren. 'Good gracious,' she exclaimed, 'I have seventy-two grandchildren, and if I were sad each time I parted from one of them, I should have a miserable existence!' 'Madre snaturale,' he replied. But speaking as one of the seventy-two, I prefer her recipe. After the age of eighty she found she had some difficulty in getting to sleep, so she habitually spent the hours from midnight to

3 a.m. in reading popular science. I do not believe that she ever had time to notice that she was growing old. This, I think, is the proper recipe for remaining young. If you have wide and keen interests and activities in which you can still be effective, you will have no reason to think about the merely statistical fact of the number of years you have already lived, still less of the probable shortness of your future.

As regards health, I have nothing useful to say as I have little experience of illness. I eat and drink whatever I like, and sleep when I cannot keep awake. I never do anything whatever on the ground that it is good for health, though in actual fact the things I like doing are mostly wholesome.

Psychologically there are two dangers to be guarded against in old age. One of these is too great an absorption in the past. One should not live in memories, in regrets for the good old days, or in sadness about friends who are dead. One's thoughts must be directed to the future, and to things about which there is something to be done. This is not always easy; one's own past is a gradually increasing weight. It is easy to think to oneself that one's emotions used to be more vivid than they are, and one's mind more keen. If this is true it should be forgotten, and if it is forgotten it will probably not be true.

The other thing to be avoided is clinging to youth in the hope of finding strength in its vitality. When your children are grown up they want to live their own lives, and if you continue to be as interested in them as you were when they were young, you are likely to become a burden to them, unless they are unusually insensible. I do not mean that one should be without interest in them, but one's interest should be contemplative and, if possible, philanthropic, but not too emotional. Animals become indifferent to their young as soon as their young can look after themselves, but human beings, owing to the length of infancy, find this less easy.

I think that a successful old age is easiest for those who have strong impersonal interests leading to suitable activities. It is in this sphere that long experience is really fruitful, and that the wisdom born of experience can be used without becoming a burden. It is no use telling grown-up children not to make mistakes, both because they will not believe you, and because mistakes are an essential part of education. But if you are one of those who are incapable of impersonal interests, you may find that your life will be empty unless you concern yourself 70 with your children and grandchildren. In that case you must realise that while you can still help them in material ways, as by making them an allowance or knitting them jumpers, you must not expect that they will enjoy your company.

Some old people are troubled by the fear of death. In the young there is a justification for this feeling. Young men who have reason to fear that they will be killed in battle may justifiably feel bitter in the thought that they have been cheated of the best things that life has to offer. But in an old man who has known human joys and sorrows, and has done 80 whatever work it was in him to do, the fear of death is somewhat ignoble. The best way to overcome it – so at least it seems to me – is to make your interests gradually wider and more impersonal, until bit by bit the walls of the ego recede, and your life becomes increasingly part of the universal life. An individual human existence should be like a river – small at first, narrowly contained within its banks, and rushing passionately past rocks and over waterfalls. Gradually the river grows wider, the banks recede, the waters flow more quietly, and in the end, without any visible break, they become part of 90 the sea, and painlessly lose their individual being. The man who, in old age, can see his life in this way, will not suffer from the fear of death, since the things he cares for will continue. And if, with the loss of vitality, weariness increases, the thought of rest will not be unwelcome. I should wish to die while still at work, knowing that others will carry on what I can no longer do, and content in the thought that what was possible has been done.

THE AUTHOR

Bertrand Russell (b.1872) is Lord Russell, but he does not use the title. He is Welsh by birth, and his grandfather was twice Prime Minister of Britain. He is a brilliant mathematician, scientist and philosopher. In 1950 he received the Nobel Prize for literature. All his life he has been a pacifist and is an active opponent of the atom bomb. Because of his strong opposition to the war of 1914–18 he was dismissed from a post as lecturer at Cambridge University and was sent to prison. He has been a professor of philosophy in Peking, and the headmaster of a progressive school in the south of England. He has written and lectured a great deal on science, sociology, psychology and the history of philosophy. In all his writings he has the gift of making even difficult subjects clear and interesting.

READING NOTES

This essay gives a good idea of Bertrand Russell's ability to instruct and entertain his readers at the same time. He is deeply sincere, but he enlivens his remarks by light and humorous illustrations.

Line 2 time of life: age.

6 *cut off:* i.e. by death. Russell makes a joke of this phrase when he repeats it in its literal meaning in line 10.

the flower of his youth: the finest part of his youth.

11 *Gibbon.* Edward Gibbon (1737–94) is famous for his *Decline and Fall of the Roman Empire.*

17 *Girton College.* The first women's college in Cambridge.

24 *madre snaturale:* what an extraordinary mother.

25 *recipe.* The instructions for making and cooking a particular dish. Here it means 'advice on how to remain young'.

28 *popular science:* i.e. books on popular science.

39 *wholesome:* good for the health.

41 *absorption:* deep interest.

48–9 *If . . . true.* This is the kind of sentence that Bertrand Russell uses in order to make us think carefully. The thought expressed in it is 'If you think you are losing your mental powers, stop thinking so and you will not lose them. If you have never thought so, you are in no danger of losing them.'

58 *become indifferent to:* lose interest in.

62 *impersonal interests:* interests that do not depend on our rela-
tions with other people. A hobby such as gardening or
photography, would be an impersonal interest.

72 *an allowance:* i.e. of money.

77 *justifiably:* rightly, with reason.

78 *cheated of:* wrongly deprived of.

80 *it was in him to do:* he had the ability to do.

83 *the walls of the ego recede:* the person becomes less self-centred.

86 *narrowly contained:* i.e. because the banks are close together.
narrowly can also mean 'only just', for example:
The boy narrowly escaped drowning when he fell into the river.
He just managed to struggle to the bank.
Notice also the expression 'a narrow escape'.

87 *passionately.* This is a human emotion applied to the river.

89 *break:* interval, pause.

EXERCISES

A. Answer these questions.

  1. 'Choose your ancestors carefully.' Why does the writer
     say this?
  2. What is Russell's recipe for remaining young? Do you
     agree with him?
  3. What are the two psychological dangers that we must
     guard against in old age?
  4. What should one do to achieve a successful old age?
  5. Who may be justifiably afraid of death, and why?
  6. How does the writer himself wish to die?

B. Choose expressions in the story to put in place of those in
italics:

  1. *My mother's father* died at the age of sixty-seven.
  2. My grandmother *spent all her time on* women's edu-
     cation.
  3. There is a good *set of instructions* for making bread in
     this cookery book.

4. Are you interested in books on *science for non-scientific readers?*
5. You need not worry about the *actual figure* of your age.
6. Old people sometimes have *too deep an interest* in the past.
7. Animals *stop taking an interest in* their young after a time.
8. Old people should try to develop *interests outside themselves and their own families.*
9. You can still help your children *by giving them things that they need.*
10. In an old man, the fear of death is *rather shameful.*

C. Write each of these sentences three times, following the model of the example.

Example: They (hear) you if you (shout).

(a) They will hear you if you shout.
(b) They would hear you if you shouted.
(c) They would have heard you if you had shouted.

1. If you (be) incapable of impersonal interests, you (find) your life empty.
2. If weariness (increase), the thought of rest (be) welcome.
3. If you (tell) them that, they (believe, *negative*) you.
4. You (become) a burden to your children if you (be) too interested in them.
5. If you (can see) your life in this way, you (suffer, *negative*).
6. You (think, *negative*) of the shortness of your future if you (have) wide interests.
7. She (read) popular science if she (can sleep, *negative*).
8. If it (be) forgotten, it (be) probably not true.
9. They (lead) an empty life unless they (concern) themselves with their children.
10. If she (be) sad each time she (part) from them, she (have) a miserable existence.

D. Complete these sentences.

1. . . . spite . . . the title, this article will really be . . . how
   not . . . grow old, which, . . . my time . . . life, is a much
   more important subject.
2. My grandfather was cut . . . . . . the flower . . . his
   youth . . . the age . . . sixty-seven.
3. Only one . . . them did not live . . . a great age, and he
   died . . . a disease which is now rare.
4. . . . her last day she remained a terror . . . all her
   descendants.
5. She worked hard . . . opening the medical profession
   . . . women.

E. Make each sentence agree with the essay, using one of the
phrases in brackets.

1. The article is really on (choosing one's ancestors, growing old, not growing old).
2. A great-grandmother of mine (entered the medical
   profession, had her head cut off, died at the age of
   ninety-two).
3. The way to remain young is to (have seventy-two
   grandchildren, have wide and keen interests, read
   popular science instead of sleeping)
4. Old people should (be indifferent to their children, become a burden to their children, let their children lead
   their own lives).
5. A successful old age is easiest for those who (develop
   their own interests, knit jumpers for their grandchildren, prevent grown-up children from making mistakes).

F. Subjects for composition and discussion:

1. 'This article will really be on how *not* to grow old.'
   Explain the author's aim in writing the article.
2. What have you learnt from this article about Bertrand
   Russell's attitude to other people and to himself?

9

The Barber Whose Uncle Had His Head Bitten Off by a Circus Tiger

WILLIAM SAROYAN

THE whole world wanted me to get a haircut. My head was too big for the world. Too much black hair, the world said. Everybody said, When are you going to get a haircut?

So finally I went to an Armenian barber on Mariposa Street named Aram who was a farmer by rights, or maybe a blacksmith, or maybe a philosopher. I didn't know. I only knew he had a little shop on Mariposa Street and spent most of his time reading Armenian papers, rolling cigarettes, smoking them, and watching the people go by. I never did see him giving anybody a haircut or a shave, although I suppose one or two people   10
went into his shop by mistake.

I went to Aram's shop on Mariposa Street and woke him up. He was sitting at the little table with an Armenian book open before him, sleeping.

In Armenian I said, Will you cut my hair? I have twenty-five cents.

Ah, he said, I am glad to see you. What is your name? Sit down. I will make coffee first. Ah, that is a fine head of hair you have.

Everybody wants me to get a haircut, I said. Can you do it?   20
Can you cut it all away, so they will not talk about it again for a long time?

Coffee, said the barber. Let us sip a little coffee first.

He brought me a cup of coffee, and I wondered how it was I had never before visited him, perhaps the most interesting

man in the whole city. I knew he was a remarkable man from
the way he wakened when I entered the store, from the way
he talked, and walked, and gestured. He was about fifty and I
was eleven. He was no taller than I was and no heavier, but his
30 face was the face of a man who has found out, who knows, who
is wise, and yet loves and is not unkind.

When he opened his eyes, his glance seemed to say, The
world? I know all about the world. Evil and miserliness, hatred
and fear, uncleanliness and rot. Even so, I love it all.

I lifted the small cup to my lips and sipped the hot black
fluid. It tasted finer than anything I had ever tasted before.

Sit down, he said in Armenian. Sit down, sit down. We have
nowhere to go. We have nothing to do. Your hair will not grow
in an hour.

40   I sat down and laughed in Armenian, and he began to tell
me about the world.

He told me about his uncle Misak who was born in Moush.

We drank the coffee and then I got into the chair and he
began to cut my hair. He gave me the worst haircut I had ever
got, much worse than the ones I got at the barber college
across the tracks, free, but he told me about his poor uncle
Misak and the circus tiger.

My poor uncle Misak, he said to me, was born a long time
ago in Moush and he was a very wild boy, although he was not
50 a thief. He was wild with people who thought they were strong
and he could wrestle any two boys in the whole city, and if
necessary their fathers and mothers at the same time. Their
grandfathers and grandmothers too, he said.

So everybody said to my poor uncle Misak, Misak, you are
strong; why won't you be a wrestler and earn money? So
Misak became a wrestler. He broke the bones of eighteen
strong men before he was twenty. And all he did with his
money was eat and drink and give the rest to children. He
didn't want money.

60   Ah, he said, that was long ago. Now everybody wants
money. They told him he would be sorry some day, and of

course they were right. They told him to take care of his
money because some day he would no longer be strong and he
would not be able to wrestle, and he would have no money.
And the day came. My poor uncle Misak was forty years old
and no longer strong, and he had no money. They laughed at
him, and he went away. He went to Constantinople. Then he
went to Vienna.

Vienna? I said. Your uncle Misak went to Vienna?

Yes, of course, said the barber. My poor uncle went to many   70
places. In Vienna, he said, my poor uncle could not find work,
and he nearly starved to death, but did he steal so much as a
loaf of bread? No, he stole nothing. Then he went to Berlin.
There, too, my poor uncle Misak nearly starved to death.

He was cutting my hair, left and right. I could see the black
hair on the floor and feel my head becoming colder and colder
with exposure. And smaller and smaller. Ah, Berlin, he said.
Streets and streets and houses and houses and people and
people, but not one door for my poor uncle Misak, not one
room, not one table, not one friend.   80

Ah, God, I said, this loneliness of man in the world. This
tragic loneliness of the living.

And, said the barber, it was the same in Paris, the same in
London, the same in New York, the same in South America, it
was the same everywhere, streets and streets, houses and
houses, doors and doors, but no place in the world for my poor
uncle Misak.

Ah, God, I prayed. Protect him, Father in heaven, protect
him.

In China, said the barber, my poor Misak met an Arab who   90
was a clown in a French circus. The Arab clown and my uncle
Misak talked together in Turkish. The clown said, Brother, are
you a lover of man and animals? And my uncle Misak said,
Brother, I love men and animals and fish and fowl and rock and
fire and water and everything seen and unseen. And the Arab
clown said, Brother, can you love even a tiger, a cruel jungle
tiger? And my uncle Misak said, Brother, my love for the cruel

jungle beast is unbounded. Ah, my uncle Misak was an unhappy man.

100   Ah, God, I said.

The Arab clown was very glad to hear about my uncle's love
for the wild beasts of the jungle, for he too was a very brave
man. Brother, he said to my uncle, could you love a tiger
enough to place your head into its yawning mouth?

Protect him, God, I prayed.

And, said Aram the barber, my uncle Misak said, Brother, I
could. And the Arab clown said, Will you join the circus?
Yesterday the tiger carelessly closed its mouth around the head
of poor Simon Perigord, and there is no longer anyone in the
110 circus with such great love for the creations of infinite God.
My poor uncle Misak was weary of the world, and he said,
Brother, I will join the circus and place my head into the
yawning mouth of God's holy tiger a dozen times a day. That
is not necessary, said the Arab clown. Twice a day will be
enough. So my poor uncle Misak joined the French circus in
China and began placing his head into the yawning mouth of
the tiger.

The circus, said the barber, travelled from China to India,
from India to Afghanistan, from Afghanistan to Persia, and
120 there, in Persia, it happened. The tiger and my poor uncle
Misak became very good friends. In Teheran, in that old
decaying city, the tiger grew savage again. It was a very hot
day, and everyone felt ugly. The tiger felt very angry and ràn
about all day. My poor uncle Misak placed his head into the
yawning mouth of the tiger, in Teheran, and he was about to
take his head out of the tiger's mouth when the tiger, full of
the ugliness of things living on the earth, clapped its jaws
together.

I got out of the chair and saw a strange person in the mirror,
130 myself. I was frightened and all my hair was gone. I paid
Aram the barber twenty-five cents and went home. Everybody
laughed at me. My brother Krikor said he had never seen such
a crazy haircut before.

It was all right, though.

All I could think about for weeks was the barber's poor uncle Misak whose head was bitten off by the circus tiger, and I looked forward to the day when I would need a haircut again, so I could go to Aram's shop and listen to his story of man on earth, lost and lonely and always in danger, the sad story of his poor uncle Misak. The sad story of every man alive. **140**

THE AUTHOR

William Saroyan (b. 1908) was born in California, USA, of Armenian parents. He began working as a newspaper boy at the age of eight. When he was thirteen he had already decided to become a writer, but after leaving school at the age of fifteen he had to work hard at a number of jobs to earn a living. His literary reputation began with the publication of a short story called 'The Daring Young Man on the Flying Trapeze' in 1934. He has written novels and plays, but he is best known as a writer of short stories.

READING NOTES

Like Somerset Maugham in *Home*, William Saroyan brings himself into this story, but only to keep the narrative moving. The background is one of the multi-racial communities that make up the population of the United States. The story is told very simply, and the reader is given an amusing impression of a barber who makes up for his lack of skill at hairdressing by his ability as a story-teller.

Line 4 *on Mariposa Street*. In British English, *in* would be used here.

5 *by rights:* if justice were done.

31 *yet:* nevertheless, in spite of this.

44–5 *I had ever got:* I had ever had. This use of *got* is colloquial.

45 *barber college:* school of hairdressing.

46 *tracks:* railway line. At one time, the railway line running through American towns often divided the richer from the poorer sections of the town. Poor boys would be glad to get a free haircut from the apprentice barbers.

49–50 *a wild boy, wild with*. In the first of these phrases, *wild* has its normal meaning of 'uncontrolled' – the opposite of 'obedient' or 'tame'. In the second phrase it is used colloquially to mean 'angry'.

51 *wrestle.* We usually say 'wrestle with'. Used by itself, the verb suggests that he not only wrestled with his opponents but beat them.

72 *so much as:* even (i.e. even such a small thing as).

120 *it happened. It* is explained in the rest of the story.

123 *ugly:* bad-tempered. Although ugly usually describes the appearance of people, it is sometimes used to speak of their feelings. A typical sentence in which it is used in this way would be: The crowd was in an ugly mood, and some stones were thrown at the police.

126 *full:* with its thoughts full.

127 *clapped.* A lively use of this word to mean 'closed suddenly'. It conveys both the quick movement of the tiger's jaws and the sharp sound that they made as they met.

135 *for weeks:* for many weeks.

137 *looked forward to:* waited eagerly for.

EXERCISES

A. Answer these questions.

   1. Why do you think that the boy had to be told by other people to go and get a haircut?
   2. What hints does the beginning of the story give about Aram's talents as a barber?
   3. How did the barber receive his young customer?
   4. What did the boy think of the barber, and why?
   5. Why did uncle Misak accept the job with the circus?
   6. Why did the boy look forward to his next haircut?

B. Find expressions in the story with the same meaning as those in italics.

   1. Aram should have been a farmer *if justice were done.*
   2. You have a *splendid growth of hair on your head.*
   3. Aram knew all about the world, *but in spite of this knowledge* he loved his fellow-men.
   4. The barber college was *over the railway line.*

5. Uncle Misak never stole *even* a loaf of bread.
6. I felt my head becoming colder and colder *as the air reached it*.
7. My love for the tiger *has no limits*.
8. Uncle Misak placed his head into the *wide-open* mouth of the tiger.
9. Everyone *was in a bad temper* because it was a very hot day.
10. *I waited eagerly* for my next haircut.

C. Rewrite these sentences using *have*, on the model of the example.

Example

A friend took my wife's photograph.
My wife had her photograph taken by a friend.

1. A tiger bit off uncle Misak's head.
2. A barber cut the boy's hair.
3. A London tailor made Priestley a suit.
4. Students at the barber college cut people's hair free.
5. The parents of many modern children pay them allowances.
6. His hostess cooked the curate's breakfast.
7. A porter carried Eveline's trunk to the steamer.
8. An executioner cut off the head of Anne Boleyn.
9. The government pays many students' college fees.
10. Their grandmother sometimes knits jumpers for my children.

D. Complete these sentences, to agree with the story.

1. People sometimes went . . . Aram's shop . . . mistake.
2. One day I went . . . and woke him . . .
3. He was sitting . . . the table, . . . an Armenian book open . . . him.
4. I knew he was a remarkable man . . . the way he gestured.
5. He had the face . . . a man who has found . . .

6. Uncle Misak nearly starved . . . death, but he did not
   steal . . . much . . . a loaf of bread.
7. My uncle loved the tiger enough to place his head . . .
   its yawning mouth.
8. The tiger had carelessly closed its mouth . . . the head
   of Simon Perigord.
9. The tiger felt ugly and ran . . . all day.
10. I thought . . . poor uncle Misak . . . weeks.

E. Put this conversation between the circus clown and Uncle
Misak into the third person, as if you were telling someone else
what they said. Use *asked, answered, said* and other suitable
verbs where necessary to connect the reported speech.

Are you a lover of men and animals?

I love men and animals and fish and fowl and rock and fire
and everything seen and unseen.

Can you love even a tiger, a cruel jungle tiger?

My love for the cruel jungle beast is unbounded.

Could you love a tiger enough to place your head into its
yawning mouth?

I could.

Will you join the circus? Yesterday the tiger carelessly closed
its mouth round the head of poor Simon Perigord, and there is
no longer anyone in the circus with such love for the infinite
creations of God.

I will join the circus and place my head in the yawning
mouth of God's holy tiger a dozen times a day.

That is not necessary. Twice a day will be enough.

F. Subjects for composition and discussion:

1. Imagine you are Uncle Misak. Tell the story of your
   early years.
2. This story is really two stories in one. What is the connection between them?
3. 'Jungle beasts should not be kept in captivity.' Give
   arguments for *or* against this opinion.

10

The Secret Life of Walter Mitty

JAMES THURBER

'WE'RE going through!' The Commander's voice was like thin ice breaking. He wore his full-dress uniform, with the heavily braided white cap pulled down naughtily over one cold grey eye. 'We can't make it, sir. There's going to be a hurricane, if you ask me.' 'I'm not asking you, Lieutenant Berg,' said the Commander. 'Throw on the power lights! Work her up to 8,500! We're going through!' The beating of the cylinders increased: ta-pocketa-pocketa-*pocketa-pocketa-pocketa*. The Commander stared at the ice forming on the pilot window. He walked over and twisted a row of complicated dials. 'Switch on 10 No. 8!' he shouted. 'Switch on No. 8!' repeated Lioutenant Berg. 'Full strength in No. 3 turret!' shouted the Commander. 'Full strength in No. 3 turret!' The crew bending to their various tasks in the huge, noisy eight-engined Navy hydroplane, looked at each other and grinned. 'The Old Man'll get us through,' they said to one another. 'The Old Man ain't afraid of Hell!' . . .

'Not so fast! You're driving too fast!' said Mrs Mitty. 'What are you driving so fast for?'

'Hmm?' said Walter Mitty. He looked at his wife, in the seat 20 beside him, with shocked astonishment. She seemed grossly unfamiliar, like a strange woman who had shouted at him in a crowd. 'You were up to fifty-five,' she said. 'You know I don't like to go more than forty. You were up to fifty-five.' Walter Mitty drove on toward Waterbury in silence, the roaring of the SN202 through the worst storm in twenty years of Navy flying fading in the distant, intimate airways of his mind.

'You're tensed up again,' said Mrs Mitty. 'It's one of your days. I wish you'd let Dr Renshaw look you over.'

30   Walter Mitty stopped the car in front of the building where his wife went to have her hair done. 'Remember to get those overshoes while I'm having my hair done.' she said. 'I don't need overshoes,' said Mitty. She put her mirror back into her bag. 'We've been all through that,' she said, getting out of the car. 'You're not a young man any longer.' He raced the engine a little. 'Why don't you wear your gloves? Have you lost your gloves?' Walter Mitty reached in a pocket and brought out the gloves. He put them on, but after she had turned and gone into the building and he had driven on to a red light, he took them

40 off again. 'Pick it up, brother!' snapped a cop as the light changed, and Mitty hastily pulled on his gloves and rushed ahead. He drove around the streets aimlessly for a time, and then he drove past the hospital on his way to the parking lot.

. . . 'It's the millionaire banker, Wellington McMillan,' said the pretty nurse. 'Yes?' said Walter Mitty, removing his gloves slowly. 'Who has the case?' 'Dr Renshaw and Dr Benbow, but there are two specialists here, Dr Remington from New York and Mr Pritchard-Mitford from London. He flew over.' A door opened down a long, cool corridor and Dr Ren-

50 shaw came out. He looked anxious and tired. 'Hello, Mitty,' he said. 'We're having the devil's own time with McMillan, the millionaire banker and close personal friend of Roosevelt. Obstreosis of the ductal tract. Tertiary. Wish you'd take a look at him.' 'Glad to,' said Mitty.

In the operating room there were whispered introductions: 'Dr Remington, Dr Mitty. Mr Pritchard-Mitford, Dr Mitty.' 'I've read your book on streptothricosis,' said Pritchard-Mitford, shaking hands. 'A brilliant performance, sir.' 'Thank you,' said Walter Mitty. 'Didn't know you were in the States,

60 Mitty,' complained Remington. 'Coals to Newcastle, bringing Mitford and me up here for a tertiary.' 'You are very kind,' said Mitty. A huge, complicated machine, connected to the operating table, with many tubes and wires, began at this

moment to go pocketa-pocketa-pocketa. 'The new anesthetizer is giving way!' shouted a young doctor. 'There's no one in the East who knows how to fix it!' 'Quiet, man!' said Mitty, in a low, cool voice. He sprang to the machine, which was now going pocketa-pocketa-queep-pocketa-queep. He began fingering delicately a row of shining dials. 'Give me a fountain pen!' he snapped. Someone handed him a fountain pen. He pulled 70 a broken piston out of the machine and put the pen in its place. That will hold for ten minutes,' he said. 'Get on with the operation.' A nurse hurried over and whispered to Renshaw, and Mitty saw the man turn pale. 'Coreopsis has set in,' said Renshaw nervously. 'If you would take over, Mitty?' Mitty looked at him and at the cowardly figure of Benbow, who drank, and at the grave, uncertain faces of the two great specialists. 'If you wish,' he said. They slipped a white gown on him; he adjusted a mask and drew on thin gloves; nurses handed him shining . . .   80

'Back it up, Mac! Look out for that Buick!' Walter Mitty suddenly put on the brakes. 'Wrong lane, Mac,' said the parking-lot attendant, looking at Mitty closely. 'Gee. Yeh,' muttered Mitty. He began carefully to back out of the lane marked 'Exit only'. 'Leave her sit there,' said the attendant. 'I'll put her away.' Mitty got out of the car. 'Hey, better leave the key.' 'Oh,' said Mitty, handing the man the ignition key. The attendant jumped into the car, backed it up with rude skill, and put it where it belonged.

They're so damn cocky, thought Walter Mitty, walking 90 along Main Street; they think they know everything. Once he had tried to take his chains off, outside New Milford, and he had got them wound around the axles. A man had had to come out and unwind them, a young grinning garageman. Since then Mrs Mitty always made him drive to a garage to have the chains taken off. The next time, he thought, I'll have my right arm in a sling, they'll see I couldn't possibly take the chains off myself. He kicked at the mud on the sidewalk. 'Overshoes,' he said to himself, and he began looking for a shoe store.

100   When he came out into the street again, with the overshoes
in a box under his arm, Walter Mitty began to wonder what
the other thing was his wife had told him to get. She had told
him twice before they set out from their house for Waterbury.
In a way he hated these weekly trips to town – he was always
getting something wrong. Kleenex, he thought, razor blades?
No. Toothpaste, toothbrush, bicarbonate, carbon, initiative,
and referendum? He gave it up. She would remember it.
'Where's the what's-its-name?' she would ask. 'Don't tell me
you forgot the what's-its-name.' A newsboy went by shouting
110 something about the Waterbury trial.

    . . . 'Perhaps this will refresh your memory.' The District
Attorney suddenly pushed a heavy automatic at the quiet
figure on the witness stand. 'Have you ever seen this before?'
Walter Mitty took the gun and examined it expertly. 'This is
my Webley-Vickers 50.80,' he said calmly. An excited buzz
ran around the courtroom. The Judge asked for order. 'You
are an expert shot with any sort of firearms, I believe?' said the
District Attorney, suggestively. 'Objection!' shouted Mitty's
attorney. 'We have shown that the defendant could not have
120 fired the shot. We have shown that he wore his right arm in a
sling on the night of the fourteenth of July.' Walter Mitty
raised his hand and the quarrelling attorneys were stilled.
'With any known make of gun,' he said evenly, 'I could have
killed Gregory Fitzhurst at three hundred feet *with my left
hand*.' Utter confusion broke out in the courtroom. A woman's
scream rose above the mad shouting and suddenly a lovely,
dark-haired girl was in Walter Mitty's arms. The District
Attorney struck at her wildly. Without rising from his chair,
Mitty let the man have it on the point of the chin. 'You
130 miserable dog!' . . .

    'Puppy biscuit,' said Walter Mitty. He stopped walking and
the buildings of Waterbury rose up out of the misty courtroom
and surrounded him again. A woman who was passing laughed.
'He said "Puppy biscuit" ', she said to her companion. 'That
man said "Puppy biscuit" to himself.' Walter Mitty hurried

on. He went into an A. & P., not the first one he came to but
a smaller one farther up the street. 'I want some biscuits for
small, young dogs,' he said to the clerk. 'Any special kind, sir?'
The greatest pistol shot in the world thought a moment. 'It
says "Puppies Bark for It" on the box,' said Walter Mitty.   140

His wife would be through at the hairdresser's in fifteen
minutes, Mitty saw in looking at his watch, unless they had
trouble drying it; sometimes they had trouble drying it. She
didn't like to get to the hotel first; she would want him to be
there waiting for her as usual. He found a big leather chair in
the hall, facing a window, and he put the overshoes and the
puppy biscuit on the floor beside it. He picked up an old copy
of *Liberty* and sank down into the chair. 'Can Germany Con-
quer the World Through the Air?' Walter Mitty looked at the
pictures of bombing planes and of ruined streets.   150

... 'The cannonading has got the wind up in young
Raleigh, sir,' said the sergeant. Captain Mitty looked up at him
through untidy hair. 'Get him to bed,' he said wearily, 'with
the others, I'll fly alone.' 'But you can't, sir,' said the sergeant
anxiously. 'It takes two men to handle that bomber and the
Archies are beating hell out of the air. Von Richtman's circus
is between here and Saulier.' 'Somebody's got to get that
ammunition store,' said Mitty. 'I'm going over. Spot of
brandy?' He poured a drink for the sergeant and one for himself. War thundered and screamed around the dugout. There   160
was a breaking of wood, and pieces of iron flew through the
room. 'A bit of a near thing,' said Captain Mitty carelessly.
'They are closing in,' said the sergeant. 'We only live once,
Sergeant,' said Mitty with his faint smile. 'Or do we?' He
poured another brandy and drank it off. 'I've never seen a man
could hold his brandy like you, sir,' said the sergeant. 'Begging
your pardon, sir.' Captain Mitty stood up and strapped on his
huge Webley-Vickers automatic. 'It's forty kilometers through
hell, sir,' said the sergeant. Mitty finished one last brandy.
'After all,' he said softly, 'What isn't?' The noise of the cannon   170
increased; there was the rat-tat-tatting of machine guns, and

from somewhere came the dangerous pocketa-pocketa-pocketa of the new flamethrowers. Walter Mitty walked to the door of the dugout humming 'Auprès de Ma Blonde'. He turned and waved to the sergeant. 'Cheerio!' he said . . .

Something struck his shoulder. 'I've been looking all over this hotel for you,' said Mrs Mitty. 'Why do you have to hide in this old chair? How did you expect me to find you?' 'Things close in,' said Walter Mitty vaguely. 'What?' Mrs Mitty said.
180 'Did you get the what's-its-name? The puppy biscuit? What's in that box?' 'Overshoes,' said Mitty. 'Couldn't you have put them on in the store?' 'I was thinking,' said Walter Mitty. 'Does it ever occur to you that I am sometimes thinking?' said he. She looked at him. 'I'm going to take your temperature when I get you home,' she said.

They went out through the revolving doors that made a faintly mocking whistling sound when you pushed them. It was two blocks to the parking lot. At the drugstore on the corner she said, 'Wait here for me. I forgot something. I won't
190 be a minute.' She was more than a minute. Walter Mitty lighted a cigarette. It began to rain, rain with snow in it. He stood against the wall of the drugstore, smoking . . . He put his shoulders back and his heels together. 'To hell with the handkerchief,' said Walter Mitty scornfully. He took one last drag on his cigarette and threw it away. Then, with that faint smile playing about his lips, he faced the firing squad; erect and motionless, proud and scornful, Walter Mitty the Undefeated, mysterious to the last.

THE AUTHOR

James Thurber (1894–1961) was born in Ohio, USA, and was educated at the State University there. He later took up journalism and became a regular contributor to the *New Yorker*, the American equivalent of the British humorous magazine *Punch*. Thurber was not only a brilliant humorous writer. He was also a brilliant cartoonist, and illustrated many of his own stories. His talent for drawing can be seen at its best in *Men, Women, and Dogs*. Amongst his best-known collections of stories are *My Life and Hard Times*, *Fables for our Time* and *The Thurber Country*.

One of his favourite subjects for drawings is a large, long-eared dog with a good-humoured yet pathetic expression on its face. This dog is in some ways the key to his stories. His own description of them in *The Thurber Country* is 'mainly humorous but with a few kind-of-sad ones mixed in'. That is perhaps the best description of his work as a whole.

In his later years he faced blindness and illness with great courage and cheerfulness. He is remembered as a gentle satirist of American life and manners, with a very human understanding of the aspects of society that he made fun of.

READING NOTES

This story has become famous both as a story and as a film. It tells how a meek American man took his wife shopping and indulged in daydreaming as he drove her round.

Line 4. We can't make it: We can't get there.

6–7 *Work her up to 8,500.* This probably means 'Force the hydroplane up to a height of 8,500 feet'; but Mitty's technical expressions should not be taken seriously. A hydroplane does not in fact fly.

8 *ta-pocketa*, etc. This imitation of the sound of machinery, suggested by the engine of Walter's car, comes in several times during the story.

15 *The Old Man.* A familiar name given to the captain of a ship, aircraft, etc., by his crew.

16 *ain't:* isn't. Uneducated speech.

23 *fifty-five:* i.e. fifty-five miles an hour.

28 *one of your days:* i.e. one of your bad days.

29 *look you over:* examine you.

34 *been through:* discussed, argued about.

35 *He raced the engine:* i.e. by pressing the accelerator. This was as much as he dared do to protest against being bullied.

40 *Pick it up:* Move on quickly.
   cop: policeman.

43 *parking lot:* car park.

53 *obstreosis*, etc. There is no need to waste time trying to find out what these words mean. They are imaginary medical terms.

60 *coals to Newcastle:* unnecessary effort. Newcastle in the north of England became famous as a port from which coal was shipped, and there would be no point in taking coal there.

74 *coreopsis.* This is a very funny imitation of medical jargon. The coreopsis is in fact a common garden flower.

76–7 *who drank:* who drank too much alcohol.

81 *Back it up:* Drive your car backwards into the parking space.
   Mac. To an American this would be a rather contemptuous way of addressing someone.

82 *lane:* the section of a roadway that cars going in a certain direction must take.

85. *Leave her sit there:* Let it stay there.

90 *cocky:* impertinent, sure of themselves.

92 *chains.* These are used on car wheels in the winter to help them travel over snow-covered roads.

105 *Kleenex:* paper tissues, used as handkerchiefs; for wiping off make-up, etc.

106 *Toothpaste*, etc. Another example of a deliberate muddle of words, showing how Walter's mind is running on.

115 *buzz:* i.e. of voices.

129 *let the man have it:* hit the man.

136 *A. & P.* Atlantic and Pacific (Store).

138 *clerk:* shop-assistant.

141 *would be through:* would have finished.

151 *got the wind up:* frightened, alarmed (slang).

156 *Archies:* anti-aircraft guns.
   circus. An expression used in the 1914–18 war of a squadron of aeroplanes under the command of a famous aviator.

158 *spot:* small drink (slang).

163 *closing in:* getting nearer.

188 *blocks.* In American English a block is a section of buildings between two streets.

195 *drag:* puff (slang).

EXERCISES

A. Answer these questions.

   1. 'She seemed grossly unfamiliar.' Why did Mrs Mitty seem like this to Walter at that moment?

2. Why do you think Walter took his gloves off when his wife's back was turned?

3. 'They think they know everything.' What did the car-park attendant know that Walter did not, and why did it make Walter angry?

4. Each of Walter's day-dreams was caused by something that happened in his real life. What was the cause of the incident of Dr Mitty?

5. Why didn't Walter go into the first A. & P. shop to buy his puppy biscuits?

6. Why did the revolving doors of the hotel seem to make a mocking sound?

B. Find expressions in the text that can be used in place of the words in italics.

1. The *Commander* isn't afraid of hell.

2. You were *driving as fast as fifty miles an hour*.

3. It's one of *those days when you behave in an odd way*.

4. It's *a waste of effort* bringing us both here.

5. One of the doctors *had the bad habit of taking too much alcohol*.

6. This will *remind you of what you have forgotten*.

7. Mitty *gave* the man *a heavy blow* on the chin.

8. His wife would *have finished* at the hairdresser's in fifteen minutes.

9. The anti-aircraft guns are *making flying terribly dangerous*.

10. I've never seen a man who could *drink as much brandy* as you can.

C. Complete these sentences with *some, any, somebody, anybody, something, anything, somewhere* or *anywhere*.

1. I want . . . biscuits for young dogs.

2. Do you want . . . special kind?

3. He couldn't find a space for his car . . . in the parking lot.

NRO—D

4. Will . . . please take these chains off my car?
5. The crew hadn't . . . idea whether they could get through or not.
6. Walter couldn't remember . . . his wife had told him to buy.
7. The witness was an expert with . . . sort of firearms.
8. From . . . came the noise of the flame-throwers.
9. We can't expect . . . to fly an aeroplane in this weather.
10. There was . . . wrong with the anesthetizer.

D. Rewrite the sentences below, using a different one of these expressions in each of them: *look all over, look at, look for, look in, look like, look lively, look on, look out for, look out on, look over*.

1. I wish you'd let Dr Renshaw examine you.
2. Be careful not to run into that Buick!
3. Commander Mitty, standing motionless at the pilot window, seemed to be a statue.
4. The French window gave a view of the garden.
5. Mrs Meadows asked me to call and talk to Uncle George.
6. The audience watched as the acrobat walked into the hall.
7. I've been trying to find you for a long time.
8. I've been searching the whole of this hotel.
9. Miss Gavan told Eveline to hurry up and serve the ladies.
10. After dinner, Jones had to examine all the family photographs.

E. Complete each sentence to agree with the story by choosing the most suitable of the expressions in brackets.

1. Mrs Mitty (got her hair done, parked the car, went for some overshoes).
2. Walter Mitty (had his arm in a sling, put his gloves on, put his overshoes on).
3. He remembered that he had to buy (a fountain pen, a newspaper, some dog biscuits).

4. The sergeant told Captain Mitty that young Raleigh had (destroyed an ammunition store, drunk too much brandy, been frightened by the enemy guns).

5. Mrs Mitty told Walter she was going to (give him a drink, put him to bed, take his temperature).

F. Subjects for composition and discussion:

1. 'Mainly humorous, but with some sadness mixed in.' Is this true of 'The Secret Life of Walter Mitty'?

2. Walter Mitty as he would have liked to be and as he appeared to other people.

3. Give examples of the way in which Thurber connects the real and imaginary incidents in the story.

11

Bella Fleace Gave a Party

EVELYN WAUGH

Part 1

MISS ANNABEL ROCHFORT-DOYLE-FLEACE, to give her
the full name under which she appeared in books of reference,
though she was known to the entire countryside as Bella
Fleace, was the last of her family. There had been Fleaces
living about Ballingar, a small market town four and a half
hours from Dublin, since the days of Strongbow: a family tree
hung in the billiard room. The present home had been built in
the middle of the eighteenth century, when the family was
still wealthy and influential. The house was in a condition of
10 fairly good repair. It could not, of course, compete with Gor-
dontown, where the American Lady Gordon had installed
electric light, central heating and a lift, or Castle Mockstock,
since Lord Mockstock had married beneath him. These were
the wonder and ridicule of the country.

It would be tiring to trace the family's gradual fall from
fortune; the Fleaces just got poorer in the way that families do
who make no effort to help themselves. In the last generation,
too, there had been many signs of eccentricity: Bella's brother,
from whom she inherited, had devoted himself to oil painting;
20 his mind was occupied only with the subject of assassination,
and before his death he had painted pictures of almost every
such incident in history from Julius Caesar to General Wilson.

It would be unnecessary to describe Bella Fleace's appearance closely, and somewhat confusing because it seemed in
contradiction to much of her character. She was over eighty,

very untidy and very red; had streaky grey hair, bits of which hung round her cheeks; her nose was large and blue-veined; her eyes pale blue, empty and mad; she had a lively smile and spoke with a marked Irish intonation. She walked with the aid of a stick, having been lamed many years back when her horse rolled her among loose stones late in a long day with the Ballingar hounds, and she had not been able to ride again. She would appear on foot and loudly criticize the conduct of the huntsmen, but every year fewer of her old friends turned out; strange faces appeared.

They knew Bella, though she did not know them. She had become a by-word in the neighbourhood, a much-valued joke.

'We saw Bella,' they would report. 'Wonder how long the old girl will last? She must be nearly ninety. My father remembers when she used to hunt – went like smoke, too.'

Indeed, Bella herself was becoming increasingly occupied with the prospect of death. In the winter before the one we are talking of, she had been extremely ill. She reappeared in April, rosy cheeked as ever, but slower in her movements and mind. She gave instructions that better attention must be paid to her father's and brother's graves, and in June, for the first time, invited her heir to visit her. She had always refused to see this young man up till now. He was an Englishman, a very distant cousin, named Banks. Bella disliked him from the moment he arrived. He had horn-rimmed spectacles and a BBC voice. One day he came to Bella bearing a pile of leather-bound volumes from the library.

'I say, did you know you had these?' he asked.

'I did,' Bella lied.

'All first editions. They must be extremely valuable.'

'You put them back where you found them.'

Later, when he wrote to thank her for his visit, he mentioned the books again. This set Bella thinking. Why should that young puppy go round the house putting a price on everything? She wasn't dead yet, Bella thought. And the more she thought of it, the more hateful it became to think of Archie

Banks carrying off her books to London. She had often heard that the books were valuable. Well, there were plenty of books in the library and she did not see why Archie Banks should profit by them. So she wrote a letter to a Dublin bookseller. He came to look through the library, and after a while he offered her a thousand for the six books. Bella was left with winter coming on and a thousand pounds in hand.

It was then that it occurred to her to give a party. There
70 were always several parties given round Ballingar at Christmas time, but of recent years Bella had not been invited to any, partly because many of her neighbours had never spoken to her, and partly because they did not think she would want to come, and partly because they would not have known what to do with her if she had. As a matter of fact she loved parties. She liked sitting down to supper in a noisy room, she liked dance music and gossip about which of the girls was pretty and who was in love with them, and she liked drink and having things brought to her by men in pink evening coats. And
80 though she tried to comfort herself with contemptuous thoughts about the ancestry of the hostesses, it annoyed her very much whenever she heard of a party given in the neighbourhood to which she was not asked.

And so it came about that, sitting with the *Irish Times* under her brother's picture of Abraham Lincoln in the theatre, Bella took it into her head to give a party. She rose immediately and limped across the room to the bell-rope. Presently her butler came into the morning-room; he wore the green apron in which he cleaned the silver.

90 'Was it yourself ringing?' he asked.

'It was, who else?'

'And I at the silver!'

'Riley,' said Bella seriously, 'I propose to give a ball at Christmas.'

'Indeed!' said her butler. 'And for what would you want to be dancing at your age?' But as Bella explained her idea, a sympathetic light began to glitter in Riley's eye.

'There's not been such a ball in the country for twenty-five years. It will cost a fortune.'

'It will cost a thousand pounds,' said Bella proudly.   100

The preparations were amazing. Seven new servants were hired in the village and set to work dusting and cleaning and polishing, clearing out furniture and pulling up carpets. Then came painters, paper-hangers and plumbers, and in a moment of enthusiasm Bella had the pillars in the hall regilded; windows were re-glazed, and the stair carpet moved so that the worn strips were less noticeable.

In all these works Bella was untiring. She limped from drawing-room to hall, down the long gallery, up the staircase, warning the hired servants, lending a hand with the lighter 110 objects of furniture, sliding, when the time came, up and down the mahogany floor of the drawing-room to work in the French chalk. She found long-forgotten services of china, went down with Riley into the cellars to count the few remaining bottles of champagne. And in the evenings, when the labourers had retired, Bella sat up far into the night turning the pages of cookery books, writing long and detailed letters to the agents for dance bands, and most important of all, drawing up her list of guests and addressing the high piles of engraved cards that stood in her desk.   120

THE AUTHOR

Evelyn Waugh (1903–66) enjoyed great popularity and success as a novelist and biographer of varied talents. His father was a publisher and his brother a novelist. After leaving Oxford University he devoted himself to writing, except during his service in the Second World War. His earliest novels, of which the best-known is *Decline and Fall*, give a satirical picture of smart society in the 1920's. After joining the Roman Catholic Church in 1930, he wrote biographies of saints and modern Catholics and a novel, *Brideshead Revisited*, in which the characters belong to an old Catholic family. This and his war books concern 'real' people and not just farcical figures. The best-known of his later books is *The Loved One*, a satire on funeral customs in the United States.

READING NOTES

It is interesting to see in this story Waugh's humorous, though not unkind, attitude to an aristocratic and eccentric old lady. In his later years, when he discouraged visitors to the country house where he lived with his aristocratic wife and six children, he was often thought eccentric. As to his style, it has been said that whatever he was writing 'his conscience would require him to find for it the exact phrase'. Notice as you read that, as one critic says, 'no long speeches are put into the mouths of his characters' and that 'he never told the reader anything that was not necessary for the strict understanding of the story'. In spite of this we have a vivid picture of Bella Fleace and her household.

Line 2 books of reference. Probably directories of important families.

5 *about.* We more often say 'round' or 'near'.

6 *Strongbow.* An English commander who fought against the Irish in the twelfth century.

family tree: diagram of the members of a family with their marriages and descendants.

7 *billiard room.* Waugh indicates without long descriptions that this was a big house since only a big house would have a special room for the large billiard table. The game is called 'billiards'.

9–10 *in a condition of fairly good repair.* The phrase 'in good (or bad) repair' means 'in good (or bad) condition'. It is used of things like houses and furniture which can be repaired, never of living things.

13 *had married beneath him.* Lord Mockstock had married a woman whose family was less distinguished than his. We guess that he had married her because she was rich.

14 *wonder and ridicule.* The neighbours admired the improvements in these gentlemen's houses and laughed at their unsuitable wives.

16 *the Fleaces just got poorer:* the Fleaces simply became poorer.

19 *inherited.* This verb usually has an object; e.g. 'She inherited the house and other family possessions.'

22 *General Wilson.* A distinguished leader in the British Army, assassinated by Irish rebels in 1922.

23 *It would be unnecessary.* Compare this with the beginning of the previous paragraph, and with the critic's comment at the beginning of these notes.

31–2 *a day with the hounds:* a day spent (fox-)hunting. Dogs used for hunting are called (fox-)hounds.

34 *huntsmen:* the men in charge of the hunt.

37 *a by-word:* a legend.

38–9 *Wonder . . . last?* I wonder how long the old lady will live?

40 *went like smoke:* rode very fast.

50 *a BBC voice.* An English, not Irish, voice with a pronunciation like that of a BBC announcer, which to Bella sounded pedantically English, as opposed to the softer Irish tones.

58 *This set Bella thinking:* this made Bella begin to think.

59 *that young puppy:* that impudent young man.

68 *in hand:* available for immediate spending.

79 *pink evening coats:* red coats worn at dances organised by foxhunters.

84 *it came about:* it happened.

85 *Abraham Lincoln.* The American President who was assassinated in a theatre in 1865.

87 *the bell-rope.* This is an old house with no electricity, and the bells are rung by pulling a rope.
butler: chief manservant. If Bella had not been poor, he would have had a footman under him to clean the silver.

90 *Was it yourself?* Irish English for 'Was it you?'

91 *who else?:* who else could it be?

95 *for what?* Irish English for 'why?'

108 *works.* The singular, *work,* is more common in this sense. In the plural we would say 'jobs' or 'activities'. *Works* is most commonly used for an author's (or artist's) works, and for good works, meaning social service or charity.

112 *mahogany.* This is a very expensive imported wood. To use it for a large floor must have cost a lot of money.

112–13 *French chalk:* a powder which is sprinkled on a dance floor to make it slippery.

113 *services:* sets of plates and dishes with the same pattern.

115 *labourers:* men who do heavy outdoor work. Here used humorously to suggest the hard work done in the house.

119 *engraved cards.* Bella had her invitations engraved on a copper plate and the cards printed from this instead of by the cheaper method of ordinary printing.

EXERCISES

A. Answer these questions.

1. Why had Bella become 'a by-word in the neighbour-hood'?
2. Why do you think Bella disliked Mr Banks?
3. Why did Bella think of selling her books? How did she arrange the sale, and what was the result?
4. What preparations did Bella make for the party?
5. How did the guests amuse themselves at the Christmas parties given by the other hostesses around Ballingar?

B. Study the story and find anything which shows:

1. how rich the family had been in the past;
2. how poor the family had become;
3. Bella's character and attitude to life.

C. Complete each sentence below, using one of the words from this list: *agent, ancestry, assassination, cellar, compete, criticise, heir, install, intonation, plumber.*

1. The ... of President Kennedy happened a hundred years after that of Abraham Lincoln.
2. We are going to ... central heating before next winter.
3. My uncle has no son, so I am ... to his estate.
4. The pipes burst in the frost, and we had to wait a week for the ...
5. She found an old family tree, which proved her distinguished ...
6. If you want to engage the dance band, you must write to their ...
7. It is not polite to ... your aunt to her face in her own house.
8. She knows a lot of English words and pronounces the sounds correctly, but her ... is unmistakably foreign.
9. My neighbour keeps wine in his ..., but I have only wood and coal in mine.

10. His children are so brilliant that no one at their school can . . . with them.

D. Find expressions in the text with the same meaning as those below:

1. directories
2. a system of radiators
3. strange behaviour
4. came to take part
5. the earliest copies of a book
6. noticing the money value of
7. get the benefit of
8. conversation about other people's private affairs
9. men who stick up wall-paper
10. put new glass in broken windows

E. Rewrite lines 87–95 without using inverted commas, beginning: Her butler came into the morning-room, wearing the green . . . the silver, and asked whether . . .

E. Rewrite these sentences, putting the words in brackets in the most suitable place.

1. The house was in a condition of good repair (fairly).
2. His mind was occupied with the subject of assassination (only).
3. It would be unnecessary to describe Bella's appearance (closely).
4. She would appear and criticise the conduct of the huntsmen (loudly).
5. Bella herself was becoming occupied with the subject of death (indeed, increasingly).
6. In the winter she had been ill (extremely).
7. She rose and limped across the room to the bell-rope (immediately).
8. Her butler came into the morning-room (presently).
9. 'Riley,' said Bella, 'I propose to give a ball at Christmas.' (seriously).
10. The stair carpet was worn (noticeably).

G. Subjects for composition and discussion:

1. Imagine you are a visitor to Ballingar. Using the information in the first two paragraphs, write to a friend who has asked you about the Fleace family. Use the present tense where appropriate.

2. If you had lived near Miss Fleace, would you have invited her to your parties? Give your reasons.

3. Write, or act with another student, a conversation between Riley and a friend of his about the preparations for the ball.

12

Bella Fleace Gave a Party

Part 2

DISTANCE counts for little in Ireland. People will readily drive three hours to pay an afternoon call, and for a dance of such importance no journey was too great. Cheerfully, in a steady childish handwriting, Bella wrote the names on her cards and addressed the envelopes. It was the work of several late sittings. Many of those whose names were written were dead or ill; some whom she just remembered seeing as small children were reaching retiring age in foreign countries, many of the houses she wrote down were blackened shells, burned during the troubles and never rebuilt. But at last, none too 10 early, the last envelope was addressed. A final job with the stamps and then later than usual, she rose from the desk. Her limbs were stiff, her eyes tired; she felt a little dizzy, but she locked her desk that evening with the knowledge that the most serious part of the work of the party was over. Several people had intentionally been left out from that list.

'What's all this I hear about Bella giving a party?' said Lady Gordon to Lady Mockstock. 'I haven't had a card.'

'Neither have I yet. I hope the old thing hasn't forgotten me. I certainly intend to go. I've never been inside the house. 20 I believe she's got some lovely things.'

As the last days approached Bella concentrated more upon her own appearance. She had bought few clothes of recent years, and the Dublin dressmaker with whom she used to deal had shut up shop. For an instant she played with the idea of a journey to London and even Paris. In the end she discovered a shop to suit her, and bought a very splendid gown of red satin; to this she added long white gloves and satin shoes. She ordered a hairdresser down from Dublin to dress her hair.

30   On the day of the ball she woke early, slightly feverish with
nervous excitement, and waited in bed till she was called,
restlessly rehearsing in her mind every detail of the arrangements. Before noon she had been to supervise the setting of
hundreds of candles round the ballroom and supper-room; she
had seen the supper tables laid out with silver and glass; she
had helped decorate the staircase and hall with chrysanthe-
mums. She had no luncheon that day. She felt a little faint; lay
down for a short time, but soon got up to sew with her own hands
the crested buttons on to the liveries of the hired servants.

40   The invitations were timed for eight o'clock. She wondered
whether that were too early – she had heard tales of parties
that began very late – but as the afternoon dragged on un-
bearably, Bella became glad she had set a short term on this
tiring wait.

At six she went up to dress. The hairdresser was there with
a bag full of combs. He brushed and curled her hair until it
became orderly and formal. She put on all her jewellery, and
standing before the glass in her room, could not stop a gasp of
surprise. Then she limped downstairs.

50   The house looked splendid in the candlelight. The band was
there, the twelve hired footmen, Riley in knee breeches and
black silk stockings.

It struck eight. Bella waited. Nobody came.

She sat down on a gilt chair at the head of the stairs, looked
steadily before her with empty, blue eyes. In the hall, in the
cloakroom, in the supper-room, the hired footmen looked
steadily at one another with knowing smiles. 'What does the
old girl expect? No one'll have finished dinner before ten.'

At half past twelve Bella rose from her chair. Her face gave
60 no sign of what she was thinking.

'Riley, I think I will have some supper. I am not feeling
altogether well.'

She limped slowly to the dining-room.

'Give me a stuffed quail and a glass of wine. Tell the band to
start playing.'

The Blue Danube waltz flooded the house. Bella smiled approval and swayed her head a little to the rhythm.

'Riley, I am really quite hungry. I've had nothing to eat all day. Give me another quail and some more champagne.'

Alone among the candles and the hired footmen, Riley 70 served his mistress with an enormous supper. She enjoyed every mouthful.

Presently she rose. 'I am afraid there must be some mistake. No one seems to be coming to the ball. It is very disappointing after all our trouble. You may tell the band to go home.'

But just as she was leaving the dining-room there was a stir in the hall. Guests were arriving. With wild resolution Bella swung herself up the stairs. She must get to the top before the guests were announced. One hand on the banister, one on her stick, beating heart, two steps at a time. At last she reached the 80 landing and turned to face the company. There was a mist before her eyes and a singing in her ears. She breathed with effort, but dimly she saw four figures advancing and saw Riley meet them and heard him announce:

'Lord and Lady Mockstock, Sir Samuel and Lady Gordon.'

Suddenly the daze in which she had been moving cleared. Here on the stairs were the two women she had not invited – Lady Mockstock the draper's daughter, Lady Gordon the American.

She drew herself up and fixed them with her empty, blue 90 eyes.

'I had not expected this honour,' she said. 'Please forgive me if I am unable to entertain you.'

The Mockstocks and the Gordons stood aghast; saw the mad blue eyes of their hostess, her red dress; the ballroom beyond, looking enormous in its emptiness; heard the dance music echoing through the empty house. The air was heavy with the scent of chrysanthemum. And then the drama and unreality of the scene disappeared. Miss Fleace suddenly sat down, and holding out her hands to her butler, said, 'I don't quite know 100 what's happening.'

He and two of the hired footmen carried the old lady to a sofa. She spoke only once more. Her mind was still on the same subject. 'They came uninvited, those two . . . and nobody else.'

A day later she died.

Mr Banks arrived for the funeral and spent a week sorting out her belongings. Among them he found in her desk, stamped, addressed, but unposted, the invitations to the ball.

READING NOTES

Line 5–6 *several late sittings.* She sat up late at her work on several evenings.

8 *were reaching retiring age in foreign countries.* Many Irish people emigrated to seek their fortunes (see 'Eveline', page 14, first note), but Bella's friends would more probably be abroad on government service.

9 *shells:* empty, burnt-out buildings.

10 *the troubles.* The name given by the Irish to the rebellion against England leading to their independence in 1922.

10–11 *none too early:* rather late.

19 *the old thing.* A familiar reference to Miss Fleace.

21 *some lovely things:* beautiful and valuable possessions.

25 *shut up shop:* retired from business.

27 *gown.* A slightly old-fashioned word for a woman's formal dress.

39 *crested:* bearing the crest or distinctive symbol of a noble family.
   liveries: the uniforms of servants.

43 *set a short term on it:* arranged for it to end early.

57 *knowing smiles.* They smiled at one another as if to say, 'We know more about parties than Miss Fleace does.'

67 *swayed:* moved backwards and forwards like a tree in the wind.

72 *mouthful.* Notice the spelling – only one *l.* Other examples of this spelling are *handful, basketful, basinful.*

85 *Sir Samuel and Lady Gordon.* Men whose title is 'Sir' are addressed as 'Sir' + first name, and spoken of as 'Sir' + first name + surname. Their wives are both addressed and spoken of as 'Lady' + surname. If you meet Sir Samuel Gordon when you visit England, call him 'Sir Samuel'. Call his wife 'Lady Gordon', not 'Lady Rebecca'.

86 *daze:* confused state of mind.
107 *her belongings:* her possessions, things that belonged to her.
108 An example of Waugh's economy of phrase. The key to the
  whole story is the one word *unposted* – six words from the end.

EXERCISES

A. Answer these questions.

  1. Why were many of Bella's invited guests unlikely to
     receive their invitations?
  2. What have you already learned about Lady Gordon and
     Lady Mockstock?
  3. What preparations did Bella make on the day of the
     ball itself?
  4. What happened after it struck eight o'clock?
  5. 'The drama and unreality of the scene disappeared.'
     Would you describe the scene to which these words refer
     as dramatic and unreal? Give reasons for your answer.

B. 1. Study both parts of the story and find everything which
      tells you that it takes place in Ireland.

   2. Make a timetable of the day of the party.

   3. Write down all the bills which had to be paid with
      Bella's £1000, including materials and labour, but
      omitting actual prices.

C. Add two more to each of these sentences to complete the
set of three pairs of tenses, as in the example.

  Example

  If I ask her she will not want to come.
  If I asked her, she would not want to come.
  If I had asked her, she would not have wanted to come.

  1. If she came, I should not know what to do with her.
  2. I cannot invite her if I have never spoken to her.
  3. If my butler announces the draper's daughter, I shall
     refuse to entertain her.

4. If Bella had posted the invitations, everyone would have accepted.
5. If I died, my nephew would sell my books.
6. If it had been a first edition, it would have been very valuable.
7. If the house is burnt down, how can the postman deliver a letter there?
8. If she were able to travel, she would buy a gown in Paris.
9. If the singing mistress receives a telegram, I shall send a message to her formroom.
10. If you want your grandchildren to love you, you will not try to arrange their lives.

D. Find expressions in the second part of the text with the same meaning as the phrases below:

1. people did not mind how far they travelled
2. several long evenings' work
3. the age when people stop working
4. on purpose
5. repeating to make sure every detail is right
6. the afternoon went by slowly
7. she walked as if her leg hurt her
8. the visitors' names were called out
9. she raised her head and stood erect
10. she was still thinking of the same thing

E. Subjects for composition and discussion:

1. Compare this story with 'Melpomenus Jones' (p. 1). Which do you prefer? Why?
2. Imagine that Bella had invited Mr Banks to stay and help her prepare for the party. Finish the story in 150 words.
3. Write or act a conversation between one of the hired footmen and his wife after the ball.
4. Describe the best party you have ever attended.

13

The Inspiration of Mr Budd

DOROTHY L. SAYERS

£500 REWARD

THE *Evening Messenger* has decided to offer the above reward to any person who shall give information leading to the arrest of the man, William Strickland, who is wanted by the police in connection with the murder of the late Emma Strickland at 59, Acacia Crescent, Manchester.

DESCRIPTION OF THE WANTED MAN

The following is the official description of William Strickland: Age 43; height 6 ft 1 or 2; complexion rather dark; hair silver-grey and abundant, may dye same; full grey moustache and beard, may now be clean-shaven; eyes light grey; left upper eye-tooth stopped with gold; left thumb-nail deformed by a recent blow.

Speaks in rather loud voice; quick, decisive manner.

Disappeared 5th inst., and may have left, or will try to leave, the country.

Mr Budd read the description through carefully once again and sighed. It was most unlikely that William Strickland should choose his small and unsuccessful saloon, out of all the barbers' shops in London, for a haircut or a shave, still less for 'dyeing same'; even if he was in London, which Mr Budd saw no reason to suppose.

Nevertheless, Mr Budd committed the description, as well as he could, to memory. It was a chance – and Mr Budd's eye was always fascinated by headlines with money in them.

He put the newspaper down, and as he did so, caught sight of his own reflection in the glass and smiled, for he was not without a sense of humour. He did not look quite the man to catch a brutal murderer single-handed. He was well on in the middle forties – with a small paunch and pale hair, five feet six at most, and soft-handed, as a hairdresser must be.

Even razor in hand, he would hardly be a match for William Strickland, height six feet one or two, who had so fiercely beaten his old aunt to death. Shaking his head doubtfully, Mr Budd advanced to the door, and nearly ran into a large customer who dived in rather suddenly.

'I beg your pardon, sir,' murmured Mr Budd, fearful of losing ninepence; 'just stepping out for a breath of fresh air, sir. Shave, sir?'

The large man tore off his overcoat without waiting for Mr Budd's helping hands.

'Are you prepared to die?' he demanded abruptly.

The question fitted in so alarmingly with Mr Budd's thoughts about murder that for a moment it quite threw him off his professional balance.

'I beg your pardon, sir,' he stammered, and in the same moment decided that the man must be a preacher of some kind. He looked rather like it, with his odd, light eyes, his bush of fiery red hair and short chin-beard.

'Do you do dyeing?' said the man impatiently.

'Oh!' said Mr Budd, relieved, 'yes, sir, certainly, sir.'

A stroke of luck, this: dyeing meant quite a big sum.

'Fact is,' said the man, 'my young lady doesn't like red hair. She says it attracts attention. Dark brown, now – that's the colour she has a fancy for. And I'm afraid the beard will have to go. My young lady doesn't like beards.'

'Will you have the moustache off as well, sir?'

'Well, no – no, I think I'll stick to that as long as I'm allowed to, what?' He laughed loudly, and Mr Budd approvingly noted well-kept teeth and a gold stopping. The customer was obviously ready to spend money on his personal appearance.

In fancy, Mr Budd saw this well-off and gentlemanly customer advising all his friends to visit 'his man'. It was most
important that there should be no failure. Hair-dyes were
awkward things – there had been a case in the paper lately.

'I see you have been using a tint before, sir,' said Mr Budd
with respect. 'Could you tell me . . .?'

'Eh?' said the man. 'Oh, yes – well, fact is, as I said, my
fiancée's a good bit younger than I am. As I expect you can see
I began to go grey early – my father was just the same – all   70
our family – so I had it touched up – grey bits restored, you
see. But she doesn't like the colour, so I thought, if I have to
dye it at all, why not a colour she *does* fancy while we're about
it, what?'

Lightly talking about the feminine mind, Mr Budd gave
his customer's hair the examination of trained eye and fingers.
Never – never in the process of nature could hair of that kind
have been red. It was naturally black hair, prematurely grey.
However, that was none of his business. He received the information he really needed – the name of the dye formerly   80
used, and noted that he would have to be careful. Some dyes
do not mix kindly with other dyes.

Chatting pleasantly, Mr Budd worked on, and as he used
the roaring drier, talked of the Manchester murder.

'The police seem to have given it up as a bad job,' said the man.

'Perhaps the reward will liven things up a bit,' said Mr
Budd, the thought being naturally uppermost in his mind.

'Oh, there's a reward, is there? I hadn't seen that.'

'It's in to-night's paper, sir. Maybe you'd like to have a look
at it.'   90

The stranger read the paragraph carefully and Mr Budd,
watching him in the glass, saw him suddenly draw back his
left hand, which was resting carelessly on the arm of the chair,
and push it under the white apron.

But not before Mr Budd had seen it. Not before he had taken
conscious note of the horny, deformed thumb-nail. Many
people had such an ugly mark, Mr Budd told himself hurriedly,

but the man glanced up, and the eyes of his reflection became fixed on Mr Budd's face in a serious examination.

100 'Well,' said Mr Budd, 'the man is safe out of the country by now, I reckon. They've put it off too late.'

The man laughed.

'I reckon they have,' he said. Mr Budd wondered whether many men with smashed left thumbs showed a gold left upper eye-tooth. Probably there were hundreds of people like that going about the country. Likewise with silver-grey hair ('may dye same') and aged about forty-three. Undoubtedly.

There came back to him the exact number and extent of the brutal wounds inflicted upon the Manchester victim – an 110 elderly lady, rather stout, she had been. Glancing through the door, Mr Budd noticed that the streets were full of people. How easy it would be . . .

'Be as quick as you can, won't you?' said the man, a little impatiently, but pleasantly enough. 'It's getting late. I'm afraid it will keep you overtime.'

'Not at all, sir,' said Mr Budd. 'It doesn't matter at all.'

No – if he tried to rush out of the door, his terrible customer would jump upon him, drag him back, and then with one frightful blow like the one he had given his aunt . . .

120 Yet surely Mr Budd was in a position of advantage. A decided man would do it. He would be out in the street before the customer could get out of the chair. Mr Budd began to move round towards the door.

'What's the matter?' said the customer.

'Just stepping out to look at the time, sir,' said Mr Budd softly and stopped. He retreated to the back of the shop, collecting his materials. If only he had been quicker – more like a detective in a book – he would have observed that thumb-nail, that tooth, put two and two together, and run out 130 to give the alarm while the man's beard was wet and soapy and his face buried in the towel. Or he could have put lather in his eyes – nobody could possibly commit a murder or even run away down the street with his eyes full of soap.

But after all, Mr Budd didn't have to arrest the man himself.

'Information leading to arrest' – those were the words. He would be able to tell them the wanted man had been there, that he would now have dark brown hair and moustache and no beard.

It was at this moment that the great Inspiration came to Mr Budd.

As he fetched a bottle from the glass-fronted case he remembered an old-fashioned wooden paper-knife that had belonged to his mother. Hand-painted, it bore the inscription 'Knowledge is Power'.

Mr Budd now felt a strange freedom and confidence; he removed the razors with an easy, natural movement, and made light conversation as he skilfully applied the dark-brown tint.

The streets were less crowded when Mr Budd let his customer out. He watched the tall figure cross Grosvenor Place and climb on to a 24 bus.

He closed the shop door, and in his turn made his way, by means of a 24, to the top of Whitehall.

Mr Budd was interviewed by an important-looking inspector in uniform, who listened very politely to his story and made him repeat very carefully about the gold tooth and the thumbnail and the hair which had been black before it was grey or red and was now dark-brown.

'But there's one thing more,' said Mr Budd – 'and I'm sure to goodness,' he added, 'I hope, sir, it is the right man because if it isn't it'll be the ruin of me . . .'

Nervously he crushed his soft hat into a ball as he leant across the table, breathlessly uttering the story of his great professional betrayal.

The *Miranda* docked at Ostend at 7 a.m. A man burst hurriedly into the cabin where the wireless operator was just taking off his headphones.

170   'Here!' he cried; 'this is to go. There's something up and the
Old Man's sent over for the police. The Consul's coming on
board. A message to the English police:

'Man on board answering to description. Ticket booked
name of Watson. Has locked himself in cabin and refuses to
come out. Insists on having hairdresser sent out to him. Have
communicated Ostend police. Await instructions.'

The Old Man with authoritative gestures cleared a way
through the excited little knot of people gathered about First
Class Cabin No. 36, for several passengers had heard of
180 'something up'. Sternly he bade the stewards and the boy to
stand away from the door. Terribly he commanded them to
hold their tongues. Four or five sailors stood watchfully at his
side. In the sudden silence, the passenger in No. 36 could be
heard pacing up and down the narrow cabin, moving things,
clattering, splashing water.

Presently came steps overhead. Six pairs of Belgian police
boots came tip-toeing down the stairs. The Old Man glanced at
the official paper held out to him and nodded.

The Old Man knocked at the door of No. 36.

190   'Who is it?' cried a harsh, sharp voice.

'The barber is here, sir, that you sent for.'

'Ah!' There was relief in the tone. 'Send him in alone, if
you please. I – I have had an accident.'

At the sound of the bolt being carefully withdrawn, the Old
Man stepped forward. The door opened a chink, and was
slammed to again, but the Old Man's boot was firmly pushed
into the opening. The policemen hurried forward. The passenger was brought out.

'Strike me pink!' screamed the boy, 'strike me pink if he
200 ain't gone green in the night!'

Green!

Not for nothing had Mr Budd studied the complicated re-
actions of chemical dyes. In the pride of his knowledge he had
set a mark on his man, to mark him out from all the billions
of this overpopulated world. Was there a port in all the world

where a murderer might slip away, with every hair on him
green as a parrot – green moustache, green eye-brows, and
that thick, springing mass of hair, vivid, flaring midsummer
green?

Mr Budd got his £500. The *Evening Messenger* published 210
the full story of his great betrayal. He trembled, fearing this
dangerous fame. Surely no one would ever come to him again.

On the next morning an enormous blue limousine rolled up
to his door. A lady, magnificent in furs and diamonds, swept
into the saloon.

'You *are* Mr Budd, aren't you?' she cried. 'The *great* Mr
Budd? Isn't it *too* wonderful? And now, *dear* Mr Budd, you
must do me a favour. You must dye my hair green, *at once.*
Now. I want to be able to say I'm the *very first* to be done by
you. I'm the Duchess of Winchester, and that awful Melcaster 220
woman is chasing me down the street – the cat!'

If you want it done, I can give you the number of Mr Budd's
parlours in Bond Street. But I understand it is a terribly expensive process.

THE AUTHOR

Dorothy L. Sayers (1893–1957) was born in Oxford and was one
of the first women to take a degree there. Her novel *Whose Body?*
was the first of a long series of successful detective stories. The hero
of all these is an aristocratic amateur detective, Lord Peter Wimsey,
whose versatile gifts reflect those of Dorothy Sayers herself. Her
play about the life of Jesus Christ, *The Man Born to be King*, has
been repeatedly broadcast. She has also produced fine translations
of Dante's *Inferno* and *Purgatorio*.

READING NOTE

In this story you will find some of the qualities which reappear in
Dorothy Sayers' longer books. The theme is murder and the hunt
for a murderer. There is observation of human character and an
interest in different social types. Especially there is accurate use of

some piece of special knowledge: here it is the trade of a clever hairdresser; in other stories the plot may depend on the chemical analysis of a poisonous fungus, or the complicated rules for ringing church bells in the English way.

Line 1 *£500*. Notice that the symbol £ comes first and the number second. This is read as 'five hundred pounds'. 'Fivepence' is written 5p.

2 *Evening Messenger*. An imaginary newspaper.

2–3 *the above reward:* the reward mentioned already (higher up the page).

3 *who shall give*. The normal form is 'who gives', even with a future meaning, 'shall give' is legal or official language.

4–5 *wanted by the police in connection with the murder*. The British police have to be careful not to suggest that a man is guilty before he is tried. So while there is doubt, they cannot say 'X is a murderer', but they can say he is 'wanted in connection with a murder' or 'helping the police with their enquiries'.

7 *Description of the wanted man*. 'Wanted' is used in this way only for someone 'wanted by the police'. For example, we say 'the house I want' not 'the wanted house'.

9–16 The language of the description is like that in a telegram. Only the words absolutely necessary for the meaning are used.

9 *6 ft 1 or 2*. Six feet one or two inches.

10 *same:* his hair. This is an official use of *same* for something already mentioned.

12 *eye-tooth:* canine tooth.
stopped: filled.

15 *inst.:* this month. Short form of *instant*, used only in official or business letters.

19 *saloon*. This is a rather old-fashioned name for a barber's shop. Modern hairdressers' shops, especially for women, are called *salons*.

23–4 *committed to memory:* learned by heart.

24 *It was a chance*. There was a possibility that Strickland would come to Mr Budd's shop.

24–5 *Mr Budd's eye was always fascinated*. A combination of two expressions; 'Mr Budd's eye was always caught' and 'Mr Budd was always fascinated'.

25 *headlines with money in them*. The headline was '£500 reward'.

28–9 *the man to catch a murderer:* the type of man who would be capable of catching a murderer.

29 *single-handed:* without help.

29–30 *well on in the middle forties:* between forty-six and forty-eight.

30 *with a small paunch.* A paunch is a fat stomach, a sign of middle age. A *small paunch* suggests that Mr Budd was beginning to get fat.

30–1 *five feet six at most:* certainly not more than five feet six inches tall, i.e. about seven inches (17 cm) shorter than Strickland.

32 *razor in hand:* with his razor in his hand.

34 *doubtfully:* anxiously, wondering what he would do if Strickland came in.

38 *ninepence.* The price of a man's haircut at the time when this story was written.

   stepping out: going a short distance, taking a few steps.

40 *tore off his overcoat:* pulled off his overcoat violently. Do not confuse with 'tore his overcoat' (made a hole in it).

44–5 *threw him off his professional balance:* upset his professional calm.

47 *preacher:* minister of religion. Mr Budd thinks his customer is asking whether he is spiritually prepared to enter the next world.

50 *Do you do dyeing?* What the customer meant by his first question was 'Are you prepared to dye (change the colour of) hair?' The words *die* and *dye* have the same sound. The wrong spelling was used in line 42 to give the reader the same wrong impression as Mr Budd received. 'Do you *do* dyeing' can only mean one thing, whether heard or read.

53 *Fact is:* the fact is.

   my young lady: my fiancée.

55 *fancy:* liking.

   I'm afraid: I am sorry to say.

57 *off:* shaved off.

58 *stick to:* keep.

62 *well-off:* rich.

63 *his man:* (here) his barber. Used also of other people who give personal service as, for example, a tailor.

65 *a case in the paper.* Probably an 'example' in the newspaper of a hairdye that went wrong. *Case* also means 'lawsuit' and a

customer might well have 'brought a case' against a barber in these circumstances.

71 *touched up:* given touches of colour where necessary. The man wants to suggest that his red hair had gone grey in parts and that he had had these dyed.

75 *the feminine mind:* the way women think.

79 *that was none of his business:* that did not concern him.

82 *kindly:* satisfactorily.

85 *given it up as a bad job:* abandoned all hope of success.

86 *liven things up a bit:* arouse interest and enthusiasm.

87 *being . . . uppermost in his mind:* being what interested him most.

96 *horny:* hard like an animal's horn.

98 *the eyes of his reflection.* Each man saw the other's eyes in the mirror watching him.

101 *I reckon:* I suppose (colloquial).

put it off too late. A mixture of two expressions: 'put it off (i.e. delayed offering the reward) until too late' and 'put it off too long'.

110 *stout:* inclined to be fat.

115 *overtime:* after closing time. As a noun *overtime* means work done outside the usual hours, or the money paid for this work.

129 *put two and two together:* drawn a logical conclusion from the evidence.

151 *Grosvenor Place:* a street near Victoria Station.

154 *Whitehall.* The street in London which passes Scotland Yard, where the police headquarters stood when this story was written.

166 *Miranda:* The name of a ship.

170 *This is to go:* this message must be sent (by wireless).

171 *Old Man.* See 'The Secret Life of Walter Mitty', page 87, note on line 15.

sent over: sent from the ship to the shore.

173 *answering:* corresponding.

178 *knot:* group.

180 *something up:* something wrong.

182 *hold their tongues:* be silent.

187 *tip-toeing:* walking as quietly as possible, on the tips of their toes.

195 *the door opened a chink:* the door opened just a little.
196 *slammed to:* shut violently.
199 *strike me pink.* A vulgar expression of surprise.
200 *ain't.* See page 7, note on line 16.
208 *flaring:* brilliant.
   midsummer. As bright as the leaves at midsummer.
211 *betrayal.* By using a dye that he knew would turn green, Mr
   Budd had betrayed his customer to the police.
213 *limousine:* a large comfortable car.
   rolled: drove smoothly and impressively.
214 *swept:* entered with dignity.
218 *green.* Mr Budd has started a new fashion.
220–1 *that awful Melcaster woman.* The Duchess of Melcaster is
   evidently a rival of the Duchess of Winchester.
223 *parlours:* a rather old-fashioned name for barbers' shops. (See
   saloon, line 19.)
223 *Bond Street.* See 'At the Tailor's', page 22, note on line 1,
   New Bond Street is part of Bond Street.

EXERCISES

A. Answer these questions.

   1. What was the *Evening Messenger* offering £500 reward
      for?
   2. Why did Mr Budd think he would hardly be a match for
      William Strickland?
   3. What did Mr Budd suppose when his customer said,
      'Are you prepared to die?' What did his customer really
      mean?
   4. What was the first thing that made Mr Budd suspect his
      customer?
   5. How did Mr Budd first think of getting help? Why did
      he change his mind?
   6. What was Mr Budd's great inspiration?
   7. What action did the captain of the *Miranda* take?
   8. What were the two ways in which Mr Budd became
      richer as a result of the happenings in this story?

B. Find expressions in the story with the same meaning as those below:

1. suspected of a crime
2. learn by heart
3. saw himself in the mirror
4. removed quickly and carelessly
5. corresponding to
6. draw conclusions
7. rich
8. while we are doing it
9. something wrong
10. to say nothing

C. Complete the sentences below, using words from this list: *awkward, complexion, deformed, headlines, inspiration, interview, overtime, restore, retreat, victim.*

1. The inscription on his mother's paper-knife gave Mr Budd his . . .
2. People from Sweden often have a fair . . .
3. His aunt was the . . . of a road accident.
4. I have only had time to glance at the . . . in the paper this morning.
5. Her hands were . . . by rheumatism.
6. The journalists waited to . . . the Prime Minister.
7. If Mr Budd had made a mistake he would be in an . . . situation.
8. He wanted the barber to . . . the colour to his grey hair.
9. The radio operator had to work . . .
10. When the passenger saw the police outside, he decided to . . . into his cabin.

D. Give the correct form of the verb in brackets in each of these sentences.

1. The barber could be seen (shave) his customer.
2. He threw down the evening paper without even (glance) at it.
3. The red-haired man was obviously ready (shoot) me.
4. If you try (force) my door open, I shall call the police.
5. The duchess saw her chauffeur (look) into the driving mirror.

6. His fiancée made him (shave) off his beard.
7. The newspaper was trying (help) the inspector.
8. His elderly aunt was so fearful of (catch) cold that she never stepped outside the front door.
9. I have decided (sell) the first editions in the library to a man from Dublin.
10. The captain saw no reason (suppose) that there could be two men with bright green hair.

E. Write sentences beginning with the expressions below:

Example

Never had he seen such an abundant head of hair.

1. Nowhere in all the world . . .
2. Scarcely . . .
3. Never in my life . . .
4. No sooner . . .
5. So unsuccessful . . .
6. Not till this moment . . .
7. . . . Neither . . . (2 sentences)
8. . . . No more . . . (2 sentences)

F. Compose telegrams of about twenty words:

1. asking a friend to meet your daughter on her arrival in England, and giving exact time, date, place and means of identification
2. to Melpomenus Jones's mother from his host, informing her of her son's death and asking her to come. Begin, 'Regret . . .'
3. to the captain of the *Miranda* from Scotland Yard, telling him to look out for Strickland and how to recognise him

G. Subjects for composition and discussion:

1. Write and act the last part of Mr Budd's interview with the inspector beginning at line 160, 'But there's one thing more . . .'

2. Give all the arguments you can think of for and against the statement that 'Knowledge is Power'.

3. Did Budd do right to 'betray' his customer? Would you say the same if he had been Strickland's dentist?

4. Describe how Mr Budd became convinced that his customer was the wanted man.

5. Show how Dorothy Sayers keeps surprises in store for her readers.

14

The Honest Man and the Devil

HILAIRE BELLOC

A MAN who was justly proud of his uncompromising temper
and love of truth had the misfortune the other night to wake
at about three o'clock in the morning and to see the Devil
standing by his bedside, who begged him that he (the Honest
Man) should sell him (the Devil) his soul.

'I will do nothing of the kind,' said the Honest Man in a
mixture of sleepiness and alarm.

'Very well,' said the Devil, obviously annoyed, 'you shall go
your way; but I warn you, if you will have nothing to do with
me I will have nothing to do with you!'   10

'I ask for nothing better,' said the Honest Man, turning over
on his right side to get to sleep again, 'I desire to follow Truth
in all her ways, and to have nothing more to do with you.'
With these words he began a sort of regular and mechanical
breathing which warned the Devil that the interview was now
at an end. The Devil, therefore, with a grunt, went out of the
bedroom and shut the door loudly behind him, shaking all the
furniture; which was a rude thing to do, but he was very
much annoyed.

Next morning the Honest Man, before going out to business,   20
dictated his letters, as he always did, into a phonograph; this
little instrument (which, by the way, had been invented by
the Devil though he did not know it) is commonly used in the
houses of the busy for the reception of dictated correspondence,
comic verse, love sonnets, and so forth. The Honest Man of
whom I speak used the phonograph for his daily correspondence,
which was enormous; he dictated his answers into it before

leaving his private house, and during the forenoon his secretary would take down those answers by reversing the machine
30 and putting it at a slower pace so that what it said could easily
go down upon the typewriter.

At about half past five the Honest Man came back from his
business, and was met by his secretary in a very nervous
fashion.

'I fear, sir,' said the secretary, 'that there must be some
mistake about your correspondence. I have taken it down
exactly, as was my duty, and certainly the voice sounded like
yours, but the letters are hardly such as I would post without
your first reading them. I have therefore not signed them in
40 your name, and have kept them to show you upon your return.
Here they are. Please read them carefully, and advise me as
soon as possible.' With these words the secretary handed the
documents to his bewildered employer, and went out of the
room with his eyes full of nervous tears.

The Honest Man put on a pair of gold spectacles, hummed
twice, then began to read. This is what he read:

I.

The Laurels,
Putney Heath, S.W.
November 9.
50

Dear Lady Whernside,
Yes, I will come to Whernside House next Thursday. I do
not know you well, and shall feel out of place among your
friends, but I need not stop long. I think that to be seen at such
a gathering, even for but a few moments, is of general advantage to my business; otherwise I should certainly not come.
One thing I beg of you, which is that you will not ask me a
number of private questions under the illusion that you are
doing me a favour. The habit is very unpleasant to me, and it
60 is the chief drawback I feel in visiting your house. I may add
that though I am of the middle classes, like your late father, I

have very good taste in furniture, and the inside of your house simply makes me sick.

I am,

Very faithfully yours,

John Roe.

II.

The Laurels,

Putney Heath, S.W.

November 9.   70

Dear Doctor Burton,

I wish you would come round this afternoon or tomorrow morning and see my oldest child, James. There is nothing whatever the matter with him, but his mother is very nervous because some children with whom he went out to a party the other evening have developed mumps, and his voice is hoarse, which she idiotically believes to a be a symptom of that disease. Your visit will cost me two guineas; but it is well worth my while to spend that sum if only to avoid her unbearable fussing. My advice to you as a man is, to look at the child's tongue, give   80 him some plain water by way of medicine, and go off again as quick as you can. Your fee will be the same in any case, and it is ridiculous to waste time over such business.

I am,

Your sincere friend,

John Roe.

III.

The Laurels,

Putney Heath, S.W.

November 9.   90

Dear Doctor Mills,

I enclose five guineas as a subscription for your new church. I confess that I do not clearly see what advantage this expenditure will do me, and I should have some difficulty in setting down in black and white my reasons for sending you the money at all. Your style of preaching is monotonous, your doctrines (if they are really your doctrines) are particularly annoying to me; and after all we could get along perfectly well with the old church. Actually I think this kind of thing is a sort 100 of blackmail; you know I cannot afford to have my name left out of your subscription list, and probably the same reason is causing many another sensible neighbour of mine to part most unwillingly with a part of his property. Perhaps the best way out of it would be to form a sort of union and to strike all together against your demands; but I cannot bother to waste any more time upon the matter, so here's your five guineas and be hanged to you!

Very faithfully and respectfully yours,
John Roe.

110   IV.
The Laurels,
Putney Heath, S.W.
November 9.

Dear Sir,

I have received your estimate for the new conservatory; I have figured it out and undoubtedly you will lose upon the contract. I therefore accept it completely and beg you to begin work as soon as possible. I fully understand your reason for making so extraordinary a bargain: you know that I shall make 120 further alterations to the house, and you hope by throwing away a sprat to catch a whale. Do not imagine that I shall make this mistake. For the next alteration I have to make I will accept the offer of some other builder as foolish as yourself, and so forth to the end of the chapter. And I am,

Your obedient servant,
John Roe.

V.

The Laurels,
Putney Heath, S.W.
November 9. 130

My dear Alice,

I will not send the small sum which you asked me as a brother to give you, though I am well aware that it would save you great worry. My reason for acting thus is that a little annoyance is caused me when I have to pay even a small sum without the chance of any possible return, and especially when I have to do it for someone who cannot make things uncomfortable for me if I refuse. I have a sort of sentimental feeling about you, because you are my sister, and therefore my refusal does give me a slight, though a passing, sense of 140 discomfort. But that will very soon disappear, and when I balance it against the definite sacrifice of a sum of money, however small, I do not hesitate for a moment. Please do not write to me again.

Your affectionate brother,
John Roe.

VI.

The Laurels,
Putney Heath, S.W.
November 9. 150

Dear Sir,

I enclose a cheque for £250, my annual subscription to the local War Chest of the Party. I beg you particularly to note that this subscription makes me the creditor of the Party to the extent of over £3,000, counting interest at one above bank rate from the first subscription. I have carefully gone into this and there can be no error. I would further have you know that I desire no reward or recognition for my payment of this sum beyond the baronetcy of which we spoke the last time I visited you, in the presence of a third party. You need not fear my 160 attitude in the approaching election; I am quite indifferent to parliamentary honours, I will take the chair five times and no more; I am prepared to attend one large garden party, three dinners, and a set of fireworks. I will have absolutely nothing to do with the printing, and I am,

> Always at your service,
> John Roe.

When the Honest Man had read these letters he decided that they should not be posted in their present form; but upon attempting to change them he found himself unable to find those phrases which he could usually discover so readily for the purpose of his correspondence.

He sent, therefore, for his secretary, and told him to re-write the letters himself according to his own judgment, which that gentleman did with great skill and speed, leaving the cheques as prepared and putting every matter in its proper light.

That night the Honest Man, who was sleeping soundly, was more annoyed than ever at the re-appearance of the Devil at his bedside in the middle of the night.

'Now,' said the Devil, 'have I brought you to your senses?'

'No,' said the Honest Man, preparing for sleep as before, 'you have not. You should have remembered that I have a secretary.'

'Oh, the devil!' said the Devil impatiently, 'one cannot be thinking of everything!' And he went out even more noisily than the night before.

In this way the Honest Man saved his soul and at the same time his face, which, if it were the less valuable of the two organs, was none the less of great importance to him in this worldly sphere.

THE AUTHOR

Hilaire Belloc (1873–1953) was born in Paris, of a French father and an English mother. He was educated in England and studied history at Oxford. After serving in the French army he became a British subject and a member of Parliament. He wrote both light and serious works, in prose and verse, on very varied subjects. He is best remembered today for his verses for children – for example, *Cautionary Tales* and *A Bad Child's Book of Beasts*, a foretaste of the now fashionable 'black humour' – and for his part in religious and sociological controversy. He was an ardent Roman Catholic and is believed to have contributed greatly to the conversion of his friend G. K. Chesterton to the Roman Catholic faith.

READING NOTES

The framework of this story is a kind of medieval legend like that of Faust about the dealings of a personal devil with a man, but the story is set in Hilaire Belloc's own day. The 'Honest Man' is revealed as an ungracious guest, an unsympathetic husband, a bad churchman and so on. It is interesting to discover, as one reads, fresh sides of his character, and, by contrast, what qualities the author admires. Belloc is clearly trying to teach us something while entertaining us.

Line 1 *uncompromising temper:* his refusal to do or say anything that was not honourable and just.

2–3 *night . . . morning. Night* includes all the hours of darkness when we expect to be asleep.

4–5 *that he . . . should sell him . . . his soul.* More correctly 'to sell him . . . his soul'.

11 *I ask for nothing better:* that is exactly what I wish.

12 *to get to sleep.* This suggests a conscious effort to go to sleep.

13 *her ways.* The idea of 'following Truth' suggests that Truth is like a person, and the possessive 'her' is used instead of 'its'.

21 *phonograph.* This is an old-fashioned word for a record-player and is not used for dictating machines.

28 *forenoon:* the later part of the morning. This word is not used in everyday English.

29 *reversing the machine:* i.e. to make it repeat aloud what it has recorded.

31 *go down upon the typewriter:* be typed out by the secretary.

37 *as was my duty.* This is a common phrase. The inversion of the ordinary word-order puts the emphasis on 'duty'.

39–40 *in your name.* When his employer was out the secretary signed the letters himself but added the words 'For John Roe'.

48 *The Laurels.* A common name for suburban houses. It suggests respectability without taste or imagination.

49 *S.W.:* South West (London).

54 *stop:* stay.

55 *but:* only.

60 *drawback:* disadvantage.

61 *late:* a formal way of referring to a dead person.

65 *very faithfully yours.* A private letter, addressing one's correspondent by name, is usually signed 'yours sincerely'.

73 *oldest.* When comparing the ages of members of the same family, we usually say 'eldest'.

73–4 *nothing whatever:* nothing at all.

76 *mumps:* a disease which causes swelling of the glands of the neck.

78 *two guineas:* two pounds ten pence. Professional men (doctors, lawyers, etc) generally used to express their fees in guineas, not pounds. One guinea = one pound five pence.

79 *fussing:* behaving in an unnecessarily anxious way.

81 *by way of:* to serve as.

83 *business.* Used vaguely to mean 'such things'. In line 20, 'business' means 'commercial work'.

91 *Doctor Mills.* The letter shows that he is probably a Doctor of Divinity (i.e. Theology).

95 *in black and white:* in writing, clearly expressed.

98 *after all:* in spite of what you say.

98 *get along:* manage.

99 *Actually:* In fact.

100 *blackmail:* money demanded with threats.

104 *union:* a trades union, an association of workers who strike (refuse to work) if they are dissatisfied.

106–7 *be hanged to you!* A strong expression of annoyance.

108 *Very faithfully and respectfully yours.* An ironic contrast with the line above.

120–1 *throwing away a sprat to catch a whale:* giving away something small in the hope of getting something more valuable in return.

123–4 *and so forth to the end of the chapter:* and so on for ever.

125 *Your obedient servant.* A formal ending, used normally by Government Departments.

142 *balance it against:* compare its importance with.

145 *Your affectionate brother.* Compare the note on line 108.

153 *local War Chest of the Party:* funds which the local branch of the political party use to get their candidate elected to parliament.

155 *counting interest at one above bank rate:* counting the interest on the money invested at one per cent above the official national rate.

159 *baronetcy:* the rank next above that of knight. Often awarded for political services.

160 *a third party:* another person.

162 *take the chair.* The person who *takes the chair* at a meeting is called *the chairman* and he controls the meeting.

164 *set:* display.

165 *printing:* i.e. of election propaganda.

169 *should not be:* ought not to be.

176–7 *putting every matter in its proper light:* giving a true view of everything. Here, of course, the secretary tactfully did the opposite.

181 *brought you to your senses:* shown you that you were wrong.

188–9 *saved . . . his face:* saved himself from embarrassment.

189 *if it were:* whether it was or not.

EXERCISES

A. Answer these questions.

    1. What did the Devil want the Honest Man to do?

    2. How did the Honest Man show the Devil that he was not wanted?

    3. How did the Honest Man get his letters written?

    4. Why did the secretary have tears in his eyes?

    5. What were the disadvantages to the Honest Man in visiting Lady Whernside?

    6. Why was Mrs Roe anxious about James?

    7. Why did the Honest Man send five guineas to the church building fund?

8. Why did he intend to have a different builder for each alteration to his house?

9. Why did he refuse a small sum of money to his sister, when he could afford to send £250 to his Party?

10. Why was he unable to change the letters he had written?

B. Find expressions in the story with the same meaning as those below:

1. not exactly of the sort that
2. disadvantage
3. two pounds ten pence
4. writing down
5. calculation of the cost
6. I have worked out the figures
7. I know quite well
8. official rate of interest
9. before a witness
10. I care nothing for

C. Complete each sentence to agree with the story by choosing the most suitable of the phrases in brackets.

1. The Honest Man (was proud and had a bad temper, prided himself upon his truthfulness, was just and loving to those in misfortune).

2. The Devil (promised to help the Honest Man, warned the Honest Man that he would never be able to sleep again, allowed the Honest Man to do as he chose).

3. The secretary (typed the letters his master had dictated, posted the letters but did not enclose the cheques, altered the letters without telling his master).

4. Lady Whernside (was an old friend of the Honest Man, invited him because he knew her father, used to ask him about his private affairs).

5. The Honest Man (wanted to save money by not having the doctor, wanted the doctor to come to satisfy his wife, thought his son was pretending to have mumps).

6. Doctor Mills (preached doctrines which he did not practise, used to blackmail members of his congregation

who had guilty secrets, asked business men to subscribe to a new church).

7. John Roe did not send his sister any money (because he did not like sacrificing a sum of money, because he was ashamed of feeling sentimental, because he thought she would worry if she were in debt to him).

8. John Roe did not change the letters he had written (because he could never find such good phrases as his secretary could, because the Devil would no longer help him to say what was untrue, because he desired to follow Truth in all her ways).

D. Complete each sentence by using one of the following phrases with the verb in the correct form: *come back, come over, go by, go off, go through, look after, look in, look up, give way, give up.*

1. As the years . . ., she often wondered if she had married the right man.

2. After trying all the week to find a jacket that fitted him properly, he decided to . . . it . . . as a bad job and wear his old one.

3. My aunt imagines that her dead husband will . . . through the open window.

4. 'Look out!' shouted the fireman, 'the roof is . . .'

5. The curate used to . . . if he was passing, and have a word with my grandfather.

6. Nearly all the young people . . . to work in the city, and the countryside is slowly dying.

7. When Michael had saved enough to buy a house in Canada, he . . . and fetched his sweetheart as he had promised.

8. I never . . . at the sun without dark glasses.

9. No cat would think of . . . its kittens once they had passed the age of six months.

10. The headmistress always . . . the ritual of disentangling her glasses before she spoke.

E. Rewrite John Roe's letter to his sister as you think the secretary would have written it.

F. Subjects for composition and discussion:

  1. A hypocrite is a man who pretends to be better than he is. Do you think the Honest Man was a hypocrite? Give reasons for your answer.

  2. Complete this letter from the local chairman of the Honest Man's political party.

     Dear Prime Minister,

         I should like to recommend Mr John Roe as a suitable man to be made a baronet next year . . .

  3. Is it better to be truthful or to be tactful?

15

The Truth about Pyecraft

H. G. WELLS

Part 1

HE sits not a dozen yards away. If I glance over my shoulder
I can see him. Poor old Pyecraft! The fattest clubman in London.

Pyecraft – I made the acquaintance of Pyecraft in this very
smoking-room. I was a young, nervous new member, and he
saw it. I was sitting alone, wishing I knew more of the members, and suddenly he came, a great rolling front of chins and
stomachs, towards me, and grunted and sat down in a chair
close by me, and then addressed me.

He talked about various things and came round to games.　10
And then about my figure and complexion. 'You ought to be
a good cricketer,' he said. I suppose I am slender, slender to
what some people would call lean, and I suppose I am rather
dark, still – I am not ashamed of having a Hindu great-
grandmother, but, for all that, I don't want casual strangers to
see through me at a glance to *her*. So that I was set against
Pyecraft from the beginning.

But he only talked about me in order to get to himself.

'I expect,' he said, 'you take no more exercise than I do, and
probably eat no less.' (Like all excessively fat people he fancied　20
he ate nothing.) 'Yet' – and he smiled a little smile – 'we
differ.'

And then he began to talk about his fatness and his fatness;
all he did for his fatness and all he was going to do for his
fatness; what people had advised him to do for his fatness and

what he had heard of people doing for fatness similar to his.
It made me feel swelled to hear him.

One stands that sort of thing once in a while at a club, but
a time came when I fancied I was standing too much. I could
30 never go into the smoking-room but he would come rolling
towards me, and sometimes he came and ate enormous meals
round and about me while I had my lunch. He seemed at
times almost to be clinging to me, almost as though he knew
that I *might* – that there was a remote, exceptional chance in
me that no one else presented.

'I'd give anything to get it down,' he would say – 'anything,' and look at me over his vast cheeks and pant.

Poor old Pyecraft! He has just gonged, no doubt to order
another buttered teacake!

40 He came to the actual thing one day. 'Our Western drugs
are anything but the last word of medical science. In the East,
I've been told –'

He stopped and stared at me. It was like being at an
aquarium.

I was quite suddenly angry with him. 'Look here,' I said,
'who told you about my great-grandmother's recipes?'

'Well?'

'Every time we've met for a week,' I said, – 'and we've met
pretty often – you've given me a broad hint or so about that
50 little secret of mine.'

'Well,' he said, 'now the cat's out of the bag, I'll admit, yes,
it is so. I heard about –'

'My great-grandmother's recipes,' I said, 'are queer things
to handle. My father was near making me promise – '

'He didn't?'

'No. But he warned me. He himself used one – once.'

'Ah! . . . But do you think – ? Suppose – suppose there did
happen to be one – '

'The things are curious documents,' I said. 'Even the smell
60 of 'em . . . No!'

But after going so far Pyecraft insisted I should go farther.

I was always a little afraid if I tried his patience too much he
would fall on me suddenly and smother me. I confess I was
weak. But I was also annoyed with Pyecraft. I had got to that
state of feeling for him that I was inclined to say, 'Well, *take*
the risk!' I didn't know much about the recipes, and, on the
whole, I was inclined to doubt their safety pretty completely.

Yet even if Pyecraft got poisoned –

I must confess the poisoning of Pyecraft struck me as an
immense undertaking.

'Look here,' said I to Pyecraft next day, and snatched the
slip away from his eager grasp.

'So far as I can make it out, this is a recipe for Loss of
Weight. ('Ah!' said Pyecraft.) I'm not absolutely sure, but I
think it's that. And if you take my advice you'll leave it alone.
Because, you know – I speak badly of them in your interest,
Pyecraft – my ancestors on that side were, so far as I can
gather, a very queer lot. See?'

'Let me try it,' said Pyecraft.

I leant back in my chair. My imagination made one mighty
effort, but gave it up. 'What in Heaven's name, Pyecraft,' I
asked, 'do you think you'll look like when you get thin?'

He would not listen to reason. I made him promise never to
say a word to me about his disgusting fatness again, whatever
happened – never, and then I handed him that little piece of
skin.

'It's nasty stuff,' I said.

'No matter,' he said, and took it.

He stared at it. 'But – but – ' he said.

He had just discovered that it wasn't English.

'To the best of my ability,' I said, 'I will do you a translation.'
I did my best.

For a month after that I saw Pyecraft constantly at the club
and as fat and anxious as ever. He kept our treaty, but at times
he broke the spirit of it by shaking his head despairingly. Then
one day in the cloak-room he said, 'Your great-grandmother – '

'Not a word against her,' I said; and he held his peace.

I could have fancied he had given it up, and I saw him one day talking to three new members about his fatness as though
100 he was in search of other recipes. And then, quite unexpectedly, his telegram came.

'For heaven's sake come. – Pyecraft.'

I got Pyecraft's address from the hall porter.

'Mr Pyecraft – ?' said I, at the front door.

They believed he was ill; he hadn't been out for two days.

'He expects me,' said I, and they sent me up.

There came a shout from inside the door: 'That Formalyn?'

'That you, Pyecraft?' I shouted, and went and banged the door.

110 'Tell the housekeeper to go away.'

I did.

Then I could hear a curious pattering upon the door, almost like someone feeling for the handle in the dark, and Pyecraft's familiar grunts.

'It's all right,' I said, 'she's gone.'

But for a long time the door didn't open.

I heard the key turn. Then Pyecraft's voice said, 'Come in.'

I turned the handle and opened the door. Naturally I expected to see Pyecraft.

120 Well, you know, he wasn't there!

THE AUTHOR

H. G. Wells (1866–1946) was the son of a shopkeeper and first worked as a draper's assistant. He later qualified as a teacher, studied hard at night school and took a degree in science. From 1893 onwards he was able to devote all his time to writing. He had a constant supply of new ideas and enthusiasms which inspired many of his contemporaries. His novels are of two kinds: realistic stories of lower-middle-class life, based on his own experience, and science fiction, of which he was a pioneer in English. *Mr Polly* and *Kipps* are examples of the first, and *The Time Machine* and *The Shape of Things to Come* of the second. Many of his stories have been filmed Wells is also remembered for his *Outline of History* and other historical and sociological writings.

READING NOTES

This story is a fantasy worked out in a matter-of-fact style which makes it seem almost probable. It is an example of Wells's humour and imagination.

Line 1 *not a dozen:* less than a dozen.

2 *clubman.* A man who is not only a member of a London club, but who spends a large part of his time there.

11–12 '*You ought to be a good cricketer.*' Pyecraft means that Formalyn (the name of the storyteller, see line 107) is slim and active and also that he is of Indian descent, and many Indians have been famous cricketers.

16 *I was set against:* I disliked.

28 *stands:* puts up with, endures.

30 *but he would come:* without his coming.

34 *that I might.* This unfinished sentence is explained by the words that follow.

36 *get it down:* reduce it (his fatness).

38 This returns to the present time as in paragraph 1.

gonged: rung the gong (to call the waiter).

41 *anything but:* certainly not. (Here *but* = except.)

43–4 *He stopped . . . aquarium.* Pyecraft looks like a fat fish staring through the glass of its tank.

49 *a broad hint:* a suggestion which is put so strongly that it is almost an open request.

51 *the cat's out of the bag:* the secret has been revealed.

60 *'em* = them. A common abbreviation in rapid speech.

72 *the slip:* the small piece of material on which the recipe was written. Line 86 suggests that it was probably parchment. 'Slip' is usually used for a small piece of paper.

73 *make out:* understand.

94 *he kept our treaty.* See lines 83–5. I made him promise . . .

97 *he held his peace:* he was silent.

98 *I could have fancied:* I almost thought.

107 and 108 *That . . .?* Colloquial form of 'Is that . . .?'

108–9 *banged the door.* This usually means 'shut the door with a bang'. Here it means 'banged (knocked loudly) *on* the door'.

EXERCISES

A. Answer these questions.

1. Where did Formalyn get to know Pyecraft?
2. How did Pyecraft know that Formalyn was partly Indian?
3. Did Pyecraft eat little in order to get thin? How do you know?
4. Why did Pyecraft talk about his fatness to his new friend?
5. Was Formalyn trying to persuade Pyecraft to try the new recipe? How do you know?
6. What were the reasons that made him lend Pyecraft the recipe?
7. Why did Pyecraft stare at the recipe when he got it?
8. What was the *treaty* that he kept?
9. What strange things did Formalyn notice before the upstairs door was opened?
10. What did Formalyn expect to see when he opened the door? What did he see?

B. Read this part of the story again and find:

1. all the references to Pyecraft's fatness
2. all you can learn about a London club
3. all the remarks intended to stop Pyecraft wanting to try the recipe

C. Find expressions in the story with the same meaning as those below:

1. people met by chance
2. occasionally
3. a very unlikely possibility
4. the highest achievement
5. a place where fish are kept

6. instructions for making food or drink
7. cover (somebody) so that (he) can't breathe
8. dangerous chance
9. accept a sensible argument
10. as well as I can

D. Use one of these expressions to complete each sentence below: *not* (or *n't*), *nothing, never, no.*

1. He sits . . . a dozen yards away.
2. I am . . . ashamed of my Hindu great-grandmother.
3. I do . . . want casual strangers to see through me at a glance to her.
4. You probably take . . . more exercise than I do, and probably eat . . . less.
5. He fancied he ate . . .
6. I could . . . go into the smoking-room but he would come rolling towards me.
7. He has just gonged, . . . doubt to order another buttered teacake!
8. I did . . . know much about the recipes.
9. I'm . . . absolutely sure.
10. '. . . matter,' he said, and took it.
11. '. . . a word against my great-grandmother,' I said.

E. Subjects for composition and discussion:

1. How would you finish these unfinished sentences in the text?

   almost as though he knew that I might . . . (33–4)
   In the East, I've been told . . . (41–2)
   I heard about . . . (52)
   My father was near making me promise . . . (54)
   Suppose – suppose there did happen to be one . . . (57–8)
   Even the smell of 'em . . . (59–60)
   Yet even if Pyecraft got poisoned . . . (68)

Then one day in the cloakroom he said, 'Your great-grandmother . . .' (95–6)

2. Would you rather be too fat or too thin? Give reasons for your answer.
3. Describe the most boring person you know, and his or her conversation.

16

The Truth about Pyecraft

Part 2

I NEVER had such a shock in my life. There was his sitting-room in a state of untidy disorder, plates and dishes among the books and writing things, and several chairs overturned, but Pyecraft –

'It's all right, old man; shut the door,' he said, and then I discovered him.

There he was, right up close to the top of the curtains in the corner by the door, as though someone had glued him to the ceiling. His face was anxious and angry. He panted and gesticulated. 'Shut the door,' he said. 'If that woman gets hold of 10 it – '

I shut the door, and went and stood away from him and stared.

'If anything gives way and you fall down,' I said, 'you'll break your neck, Pyecraft.'

'I wish I could,' he panted.

'A man of your age and weight getting up to childish gymnastics – '

'Don't,' he said, and looked agonized. 'Your damned great-grandmother – '   20

'Be careful,' I warned him.

'I'll tell you,' he said, and gesticulated.

'But how are you holding on up there?'

And then abruptly I realized that he was not holding on at all, that he was floating up there – just as a gas-filled balloon might have floated in the same position. He began to struggle to push himself away from the ceiling and to climb down the wall to me. 'It's that prescription,' he panted, as he did so. 'Your great-gran – '

30 'No!' I cried.

He took hold of a framed picture rather carelessly as he spoke and it gave way, and he flew back to the ceiling again, while the picture smashed on to the sofa. Bump he went against the ceiling.

It was really a most extraordinary spectacle, that great, fat, apoplectic-looking man upside down and trying to get from the ceiling to the floor. 'That prescription,' he said. 'Too successful.'

'How?'

40 'Loss of weight – almost complete.'

And then, of course, I understood.

'By Jove, Pyecraft,' said I, 'what you wanted was a cure for fatness! But you always called it weight. You *would* call it weight.'

Somehow I was extremely delighted. I quite liked Pyecraft for the time. 'Let me help you' I said, and took his hand and pulled him down. He kicked about, trying to get a foothold somewhere. It was very like holding a flag on a windy day.

'That table,' he said, pointing, 'is solid mahogany and very 50 heavy. If you can put me under that – '

I did, and there he rolled about like a captive balloon, while I stood on his carpet and talked to him.

I lit a cigar. 'Tell me,' I said, 'what happened?'

'I took it,' he said.

'How did it taste?'

'Oh, *beastly*!'

I should fancy they all did.

'I took a little sip first.'

'Yes?'

60 'And as I felt lighter and better after an hour, I decided to take it all.'

'My dear Pyecraft!'

'I held my nose,' he explained. 'And then I kept on getting lighter and lighter – and helpless, you know.'

He gave way suddenly to a burst of passion. 'What the goodness am I to *do*?' he said.

'There's one thing pretty evident,' I said, 'that you mustn't do. If you go out of doors you'll go up and up.' I waved an arm upward.

'I suppose it will wear off?' 70

I shook my head. 'I don't think you can count on that,' I said.

And then there was another burst of passion, and he kicked out at the chairs and banged the floor. He behaved just as I should have expected a great, fat, spoilt man to behave under difficult circumstances – that is to say, very badly. He spoke of me and my great-grandmother in a most insulting manner.

'I never asked you to take the stuff,' I said.

I pointed out to him that this was a trouble he had brought upon himself, and that it almost seemed like poetical justice. 80 He had eaten too much. This he disputed, and for a time we argued the point.

He became noisy and violent, so I left this aspect of his lesson. 'And then,' said I, 'you committed the sin of euphemism. You called it, not Fat, which is just and simple, but Weight. You – '

He interrupted to say that he recognized all that. What was he to *do*?

I suggested he should get used to his new condition.

'I can't sleep,' he said. 90

But there was no great difficulty. It was quite possible, I pointed out, to make up a bed under a wire mattress, fasten the underthings on with tapes, and have a blanket, sheet, and coverlet to button at the side. He would have to confide in his house-keeper, I said; and after some arguments, he agreed to that. (Afterwards it was quite delightful to see the beautifully matter-of-fact way with which the good lady took all these amazing arrangements.) He could have a library ladder in his room, and all his meals could be laid on the top of his bookcase.

100 He could get to the floor whenever he wanted simply by putting the British Encyclopaedia (tenth edition) on the top of his open shelves. He just pulled out a couple of volumes and held on, and down he came.

As we got on with the thing I found myself almost keenly interested. In fact, I spent two whole days at his flat. I am a handy sort of man with a screwdriver, and I made all sorts of clever arrangements for him – ran a wire to bring his bells within reach, turned all his electric lights up instead of down, and so on. It was delightful to think of Pyecraft like some

110 great, fat blow-fly, crawling about on his ceiling and climbing round the top of his doors from one room to another, and never, never, never coming to the club any more . . .

Then, you know, my fatal cleverness got the better of me. I was sitting by his fire drinking his whisky, and he was up in his favourite corner by the top of the curtain, nailing a carpet to the ceiling, when the idea struck me. 'By Jove, Pyecraft!' I said, 'all this is quite unnecessary.'

And before I could realize the complete consequence of my idea I blurted it out. 'Lead underclothing,' said I, and the

120 mischief was done.

Pyecraft received the thing almost in tears. 'To be right ways up again – ' he said.

I gave him the whole secret before I saw where it would take me. 'Buy sheet lead,' I said, 'stamp it into disks. Sew 'em all over your underclothes until you have enough. Have lead-soled boots, carry a bag of solid lead, and the thing is done! Instead of being a prisoner here you may go abroad again, Pyecraft! You may travel – '

A still happier idea came to me. 'You need never fear a

130 ship-wreck. All you need do is just slip off some or all of your clothes, take the necessary amount of luggage in your hand, and float up in the air – '

In his emotion he dropped the hammer within an inch of

my head. 'By Jove!' he said, 'I shall be able to come back to the club again.'

This was a shock. 'By Jove!' I said, faintly. 'Yes. Of course – you will.'

He did. He does. There he sits behind me now stuffing – as I live! – a third lot of buttered teacake. And no one in the whole world knows – except his housekeeper and me – that he 140 weighs practically nothing; that he is mere clouds in clothing, and the most inconsiderable of men. There he sits watching until I have done this writing. Then, if he can, he will stop me. He will come rolling up to me. . . .

He will tell me over again all about it. How it feels, how it doesn't feel, how he sometimes hopes it is passing off a little. And always somewhere in that fat, long talk, he will say, 'The secret's keeping, eh? If anyone knew of it – I should be so ashamed. . . . Makes a fellow look such a fool, you know. Crawling about on the ceiling and all that . . .' 150

READING NOTES

Line 5 old man. A term of friendship, nothing to do with age.
10–11 *If that woman gets hold of it:* if my housekeeper discovers my secret.
14 *gives way:* breaks, collapses.
17 *getting up to:* playing at.
33 *smashed on to:* fell heavily on to.
46 *for the time:* for a little while.
57 *they all did:* all the medicines from those recipes tasted beastly.
63 *I held my nose.* Medicine is supposed not to taste so bad if the patient holds his nose while he drinks it.
65 *gave way to:* surrendered to, i.e. his feelings were too strong for him, so he had to express them.
67 *pretty:* fairly.
70 *wear off:* disappear as time passes.
71 *count on:* be sure of.
80 *poetical justice.* The usual phrase is 'poetic justice', meaning the ideal state of affairs, as one might find in a poem, where all punishment is exactly what is deserved.

84 *euphemism:* calling an ugly thing by a less ugly name. It is described here as a sin because Pyecraft is not perfectly truthful.

93 *underthings:* blanket and sheet between the mattress and the sleeper. They will, of course, be on top of Pyecraft.

106 *handy:* skilful, useful.

113 *my fatal cleverness:* Formalyn's clever idea is fatal to his own happiness. See lines 109–12.

119 *blurted it out:* said it aloud without thinking of the consequences.

138–9 *as I live.* I swear it is true, i.e. it is as true as the fact that I am living.

142 *inconsiderable:* too small to be worth considering. Usually refers to character or position, not weight.

146 *passing off:* growing less, going away. Compare *wear off* (line 70).

147–8 *The secret's keeping:* the secret has not been told.

EXERCISES

A. Answer these questions.

1. What did Formalyn see when he opened the door of Pyecraft's room?
2. Why did Pyecraft say, 'Shut the door'?
3. What did Formalyn think Pyecraft was doing?
4. 'That prescription,' he said. 'Too successful.' What did Pyecraft mean?
5. What two sins did Formalyn consider Pyecraft had committed?
6. What arrangements did Formalyn make for Pyecraft to sleep?
7. How was Pyecraft going to eat?
8. How did all these arrangements become unnecessary?
9. Why should Pyecraft take off his clothes in case of shipwreck?
10. Did Pyecraft learn from his unpleasant experience? How do you know?

B. Find expressions in the text with the same meaning as those below:

1. stuck him fast
2. waved his arms about
3. the wrong way up
4. a taste of liquid
5. fit of rage
6. very rudely
7. I explained
8. to tell his secret to
9. was too strong for me
10. hardly anything

C. Complete these unfinished sentences from the text.

1. If that woman gets hold of it . . .
2. Your damned great-grandmother . . .
3. A man of your age and weight getting up to childish gymnastics . . .
4. If you can put me under that . . .
5. To be right ways up again . . .

D. Look through the story and find:

1. Formalyn's different feelings about Pyecraft
2. the things to which Pyecraft is compared
3. the exclamations used (e.g. for heaven's sake)

E. Complete these sentences with the right form of the verb in brackets.

1. You ought (be) a good cricketer.
2. I don't want strangers (see) through me at a glance.
3. He told me what people had advised him (do) for his fatness and what he had heard of people (do) for their fatness.
4. I could never (go) into the smoking-room without his (come) (speak) to me.
5. He seemed at times almost (cling) to me.
6. He had just gonged (order) another teacake.
7. My great-grandmother's recipes are queer things (handle).
8. I kept on (get) lighter.

9. Instead of (be) a prisoner here you may (go) abroad again.

10. All you need (do) is (slip) off some of your clothes.

F. Subjects for composition and discussion:

1. Compare the story with 'The Honest Man', page 121. In what ways are the stories alike and not alike? Say which story you prefer, and why.

2. Write a description of Pyecraft's room after Formalyn had spent two days working there.

3. Make up another story about a punishment that fitted the crime.

17

While the Auto Waits

O. HENRY

PROMPTLY at the beginning of twilight, came again to that quiet corner of that quiet, small park the girl in gray. She sat upon a bench and read a book, for there was yet to come a half hour in which print could be read.

To repeat: Her dress was gray, and plain but perfect in style and fit. A large-meshed veil imprisoned her hat and a face that shone through it with a calm and unconscious beauty. She had come there at the same hour on the previous day, and on the day before that; and there was one who knew it.

The young man who knew it was waiting near by. His patience was rewarded, for, in turning a page, her book slipped from her fingers and bounded from the bench a full yard away.

The young man seized it with great audacity, returning it to its owner with a look of gallantry and hope. In a pleasant voice, he risked a simple remark upon the weather – that introductory subject responsible for so much of the world's unhappiness – and stood by for a moment, awaiting his fate.

The girl looked him over leisurely; at his ordinary neat dress and his features that showed no particular expression.

'You may sit down, if you like,' she said, in a full, slow contralto. 'Really, I would like to have you do so. The light is too bad for reading. I would prefer to talk.'

He slid upon the seat by her side with politeness.

'Do you know,' he said, speaking the formula with which park chairmen open their meetings, 'that you are quite the most beautiful girl I have seen in a long time? I had my eye on you yesterday. Didn't know somebody was knocked down by those pretty lamps of yours, did you, honeysuckle?'

30   'Whoever you are,' said the girl in icy tones, 'you must remember that I am a lady. I will excuse the remark you have just made because the mistake was, doubtless, not an unnatural one – in your circle. I asked you to sit down; if the invitation must make me your honeysuckle, consider it withdrawn.'

'I earnestly beg your pardon,' pleaded the young man. 'It was my fault, you know, – I mean, there are girls in parks, you know – that is, of course, you don't know, but – '

'Abandon the subject, if you please. Of course I know. Now,
40   tell me about these people passing and crowding, each way, along these paths. Where are they going? Why do they hurry so? Are they happy?'

The young man could not guess the rôle he would be expected to play. 'It *is* interesting to watch them,' he replied. 'It's the wonderful drama of life. Some are going to supper and some to – er – other places. One wonders what their histories are.'

'I do not,' said the girl; 'I am not so curious. I come here to sit because here, only, can I be near the great, common,
50   beating heart of humanity. My part in life is played where its beats are never felt. Can you guess why I spoke to you, Mr – ?'

'Parkenstacker,' said the young man. Then he looked eager and hopeful.

'No,' said the girl, holding up a slender finger, and smiling slightly. 'You would recognize it immediately. It is impossible to keep one's name out of print. Or even one's portrait. This veil and this hat of my maid's hide my identity. You should have seen the chauffeur stare at it when he thought I did not see. Frankly, there are five or six names that belong in the
60   holy of holies, and mine, by accident of birth, is one of them. I spoke to you, Mr Stackenpot – '

'Parkenstacker,' corrected the young man, modestly.

' – Mr Parkenstacker, because I wanted to talk, for once,

with a natural man – one unspoiled by wealth and supposed
social superiority. Oh! you do not know how weary I am of it –
money, money, money! And of the men who surround me,
dancing like dolls all cut by the same pattern. I am sick of
pleasure, of jewels, of travel, of society, of luxuries of all kinds.'

'I always had an idea,' uttered the young man, hesitatingly,
'that money must be a pretty good thing.'   70

'Enough money for living comfortably is to be desired. But
when you have so many millions that – !' She concluded the
sentence with a gesture of despair. 'It is the monotony of it,'
she continued, 'that bores. Drives, dinners, theatres, balls,
suppers, with the gilding of too much wealth over it all. Sometimes the very tinkle of the ice in my champagne glass nearly
drives me mad.'

Mr Parkenstacker looked frankly interested.

'I have always liked,' he said, 'to read and hear about the
ways of wealthy and fashionable folks. I suppose I am a bit of a   80
snob. But I like to have my information accurate. Now, I had
formed the opinion that champagne is cooled in the bottle and
not by placing ice in the glass.'

The girl gave a musical laugh of real amusement.

'You should know,' she explained, in a patient tone, that
we of the non-useful class depend for our amusement upon
change. Just now it is the fashion to put ice in champagne.
The idea was originated by a visiting Prince of Tartary while
dining at the Waldorf. It will soon give way to some other new
idea. Just as at a dinner party this week on Madison Avenue a   90
green glove was laid by the plate of each guest to be put on
and used while eating olives.'

'I see,' admitted the young man, humbly. 'These special
amusements of the inner circle do not become known to the
common public.'

'Sometimes,' continued the girl, acknowledging his con-
fession of error by a slight bow, 'I have thought that if I ever
should love a man it would be one of lowly station. One who is
a worker and not a drone. But, doubtless, the demands of caste

100 and wealth will be stronger than my wishes. What is it that makes me tell you these things, Mr Packenstarker?'

'Parkenstacker,' breathed the young man. 'Indeed, you cannot know how much I appreciate your confidences.'

The girl regarded him with the calm, impersonal look that befitted the difference in their stations.

'What is your line of business, Mr Parkenstacker?' she asked.

'A very humble one. But I hope to rise in the world. Were you really in earnest when you said that you could love a man of lowly position?'

110 'Indeed I was. But I said "might". There is a Grand Duke and a Marquis pursuing me. Yes; no position could be too humble were the man what I would wish him to be.'

'I work,' declared Mr Parkenstacker, 'in a restaurant.'

The girl shrank slightly.

'Not as a waiter?' she said, almost pleading. 'Labour is noble, but, – personal service, you know – valets and – '

'I am not a waiter. I am cashier in' – on the street they faced beyond the opposite side of the park was the brilliant electric sign 'RESTAURANT' – 'I am cashier in that 120 restaurant you see there.'

The girl glanced at a tiny watch set in a bracelet upon her left wrist, and rose, hurriedly. She pushed her book into a glittering bag, for which, however, the book was too large.

'Why are you not at work?' she asked.

'I am on the night turn,' said the young man; 'it is yet an huor before my period begins. May I not hope to see you again?'

'I do not know. Perhaps – but the fancy may not seize me again. I must go quickly now. There is a dinner, and a box at 130 the play – and oh! the same old round. Perhaps you noticed an automobile at the upper corner of the park as you came. One with a white body.'

'And red wheels?' asked the young man, frowning thoughtfully.

'Yes, I always come in that. Pierre waits for me there. He

supposes me to be shopping in the department store across the square. Imagine a life wherein we must deceive even our chauffeurs. Goodnight.'

'But it is dark now,' said Mr Parkenstacker, 'and the park is full of rude men. May I not walk – ?'   140

'If you have the slightest regard for my wishes,' said the girl, firmly, 'you will remain at this bench for ten minutes after I have left. I do not mean to accuse you, but you are probably aware that autos generally bear the monogram of their owner. Again, good-night.'

Swift and stately she moved away through the dusk. The young man watched her graceful form as she reached the pavement at the park's edge, and turned up along it toward the corner where stood the automobile. Then he treacherously and unhesitatingly began to slide along the park trees and 150 bushes in a course parallel to her route, keeping her well in sight.

When she reached the corner she turned her head to glance at the motor car, and then passed it, continuing on across the street. Sheltered behind a standing cab, the young man followed her movements closely with his eyes. Passing down the sidewalk of the street opposite the park, she entered the restaurant with the blazing sign. The place was one of those glaring establishments, all white paint and glass, where one may dine cheaply. The girl entered the restaurant and went 160 to some place at the back, whence she quickly returned without her hat and veil.

The cashier's desk was well to the front. A red-haired girl on the stool climbed down, glancing pointedly at the clock as she did so. The girl in gray mounted in her place.

The young man pushed his hands into his pockets and walked slowly back along the sidewalk. At the corner his foot struck a small, paper-covered volume lying there. By its picturesque cover he recognised it as the book the girl had been reading. He picked it up carelessly, and saw that its title was 170 *New Arabian Nights*, the author being of the name of

Stevenson. He dropped it again upon the grass, and stood, hesitating, for a minute. Then he stepped into the automobile, reclined upon the cushions, and said two words to the chauffeur:

'Club, Henri.'

THE AUTHOR

O. Henry was the pen-name of William Sydney Porter (1862–1910), one of the most famous of American short-story writers. He was the son of a doctor, but led an unsettled life in his early years, working successively as his father's dispenser, a Texas ranch hand and a bank cashier. Whilst in this last employment he was accused of embezzlement of bank funds. He fled to South America to escape arrest, but returned on hearing that his wife was ill. He was arrested and sentenced to five years in prison. On his release he lived in extreme poverty in New York, drinking heavily and writing short stories to support himself. He died of consumption.

Although his life was a tragic one, it gave him a profound knowledge of human character, especially of dwellers in big cities who are unfortunate in life. As a story-teller, he is remarkable for his ingenuity in the use of ironical coincidences and for his skilful plots. In 1918 the American Society of Letters honoured his name by founding the O. Henry Memorial Award, which gives an annual prize for the best American short story.

READING NOTES

O. Henry was particularly clever at writing stories with an unexpected ending to them. 'While the Auto Waits' is a good example of this kind of story.

Line 2 the girl in gray. This is the subject of *came* (line 1). It is put at the end of the sentence to give it special emphasis. This kind of inversion is rather too melodramatic for modern tastes. It would be more natural nowadays to say 'there came', and O. Henry has used *there* in a similar construction in the next sentence *there was yet to come a half hour. gray* is an American spelling of 'grey'.

9 *one:* one person.

16 *risked.* The young man was not certain whether the girl would be willing to answer him or whether she would be offended at being spoken to by a stranger.

25–6 *the formula with which park chairmen open their meetings.* This phrase shows the realism and sophistication of O. Henry. *chairmen* and *meeting* are used in a punning sense. The title of a person who presides formally at a public meeting is here transferred to the kind of man who sits down beside unaccompanied girls and tries to scrape up an acquaintance with them.

27 *in a long time.* A colloquial, American usage. In British English it would be 'for a long time'.

28 *Didn't know:* you didn't know.

29 *lamps.* Slang for 'eyes'. This, and the word *honeysuckle* in the same line, are the kind of language the young man believes suitable for a girl who would be willing to let him make advances to her.

56 *one's name . . . one's portrait.* The use of *one's* for 'my' is intended by the girl to emphasise her high position in life.

60 *the holy of holies:* the very small and select group of people who are the leaders of society. (Literally, the holiest part of a temple.)

67 *sick of:* tired of.

74 *bores:* i.e. 'bores me (and people like me)'.

94 *the inner circle.* Another way of describing the leaders of society.

98 *one of lowly station:* a humble person. This is an old-fashioned phrase and suggests that the young lady has been reading romantic fiction.

99 *drone:* idle person. Literally, a male bee, which does no work.

112 *were the man:* if the man were.

125–6 *it is yet an hour:* there is still an hour. This is also the kind of speech we might find in romantic fiction.

130 *round:* i.e. 'round of social activities'.

157 *sidewalk.* An American expression. In British English, 'pavement'.

159 *glaring:* brightly-lit, dazzling.

164 *glancing pointedly at the clock.* In order to call the attention of the girl in gray to the fact that she was late.

171 *New Arabian Nights.* This is a collection of short stories by the British writer Robert Louis Stevenson (1850–1894). The principal character in them is Prince Florizel of Bohemia who goes in disguise amongst his subjects and is involved in a series of fantastic adventures. No doubt this book gave the girl her idea of posing as a society lady mixing with humble people.

EXERCISES

A. Answer these questions.

1. What subject did the young man choose for his first remark to the girl in gray?
2. Why did he change his manner of speaking to her?
3. What did the girl want him to tell her about?
4. What reason did she give for not telling him who she was?
5. What did she say about her way of life and her attitude to it?
6. What did the young man tell her about his position in life and why did he tell her this?
7. Why did she ask him to stay in the park when she left?
8. How did the other girl make clear to her that she was late on duty?
9. What is the significance in the story of the book that she had been reading?
10. What does the last sentence of the story tell us about the young man?

B. Find expressions in the text with the same meaning as those below.

1. very boldly
2. waiting to see what would happen to him
3. to avoid newspaper publicity
4. a person with too much respect for money and position
5. I like to get my facts right
6. the highest levels of society

7. an idle person
8. to get on in life
9. the same boring series of activities
10. leaned back in comfort

C. Write this passage in indirect speech. (Begin with *She said that . . .*)

'It is impossible to keep one's name out of print. This veil and this hat of my maid's hide my identity. You should have seen the chauffeur stare at it when he thought I did not see. There are five or six names that belong to the holy of holies, and mine, by accident of birth, is one of them. I spoke to you because I wanted to talk for once with a natural man. Oh! You do not know how weary I am of it – money, money, money. And of the men who surround me, dancing like dolls all cut by the same pattern. I am sick of pleasure, of jewels, of travel, of society, of luxuries of all kinds.'

D. Read through the story again and find examples:
(a) of the ways in which the girl in grey tries to impress the young man with her high social position
(b) of mistakes she makes which show that she is only pretending

E. Use a verb from this list to give the meaning of the expressions in italics in each of the following sentences: *can, could, may, might, must, should, would.*

1. She *would be able to* read for another half hour.
2. The young man spoke to her and stood for a moment, wondering what she *was going to* answer.
3. He asked if he *had her permission to* sit on the seat beside her.
4. 'You *have my permission* if you like,' she answered graciously.
5. You *have to* remember that I am a lady.

6. The park is the only place where I *find it possible to* meet ordinary working men and women.
7. *Are* you *able to* guess why I spoke to you?
8. You *ought to* have seen the chauffeur stare at my hat.
9. I always thought that money *would surely* be a pretty good thing.
10. The young man wanted to accompany her to her car, in case one of those rude men *happened to* speak to her.

F. Subjects for composition and discussion:

1. What has this story in common with 'The Secret Life of Walter Mitty' (page 81)?
2. Who, in your opinion, has the more attractive character, Walter Mitty or the girl in gray?
3. How does this story illustrate O. Henry's ability to invent and work out a clever plot?
4. Have you ever been tempted to pretend that you were someone else? Say what happened.
5. These are two tests of a good 'surprise' ending:

   (a) you should not be able to see it coming;
   (b) when you think over the story again, you realise that you should have seen it coming, as there were plenty of clues.

   Does 'While the Auto Waits' satisfy these tests? What clues to the ending are given?

18

Among the Dahlias

WILLIAM SANSOM

THE ZOO was almost empty. It was a day in late September, dry
and warm, quiet with sunshine. The school-holidays were over.
And it was a Monday afternoon – most people had a weekend's
enjoyment on their consciences and would forbear to appear
until Tuesday.

An exception to this was John Doole. He could be seen
at about two o'clock making his way quietly past the owl-
houses.

Doole is what may too easily be called an 'ordinary' man, a
man who has conformed in certain social appearances and   10
comportments for a common good; but a man who is still alive
with dreams, desires, whims, fancies, hates and loves – none
particularly strong or frequent. The effect of a life of quiet
conformity had been to keep such impulses precisely in their
place as dreams or desires, writing them off as impracticable.

Doole would also have been called a phlegmatic man: at
least, the opposite to a nervous type. When Doole com-
pulsively whistled to himself, or pulled up the brace of his
trousers with his left hand while his right patted the back of
his head, or took unnecessarily deep breaths while waiting for   20
a train, so deep that he seemed to be saying Hum-ha, Hum-ha
with his mouth contorted into a most peculiar shape, or went
through a dozen other such queer acrobatics during the course
of his day – these gestures were never recognised as the symp-
toms of nervous unbalance, for too many other people did
exactly the same, and Doole knew this too, he found nothing
odd in such antics.

Doole was a man of forty, with a happy pink face and receding fair hair, a little paunch, and creased baby-fat round his wrists. He wore a richly sober brown suit, a little rounded over his short figure; an eyeglass bounced on a black ribbon against his paunch; his tawny shoes were brilliantly shined.

He was in business, in fireplaces. But he would often take a walk in the afternoon between two and three. 'Nobody comes back from lunch till three, you might as well not have a telephone,' so he often said. 'I'm damned if I'm going to sit there like a stuffed dummy while they stuff the real man.' He himself was principally a vegetarian, ate lightly and often alone. He loved animals. He often visited the zoo, though he shuddered a little at the hunks of raw meat dribbling from the vulture's beak and the red bones lying about the lion's cage.

Now he stood for a moment discussing a large white owl. The owl had its trousered legs placed neatly together. Unconsciously Doole moved his own into a similar position: at any moment the two might have clicked heels and bowed. 'Just a flying puss,' Doole said to himself, considering the owl's catface of night eyes and furry ears and feathered round cheeks. 'Likes mice like puss, too,' he thought with satisfaction, forgetting in the pleasure of this observation his vegetarian principles. It is satisfactory to come across a common coincidence in the flesh – and Doole expanded for a moment as he nodded, 'How true!' As if to please him, the owl opened its beak and made, from a distance deep inside the vase of feathers, a thin mewing sound.

Doole smiled and passed on. All seemed very right with the world. Creatures were *really* so extraordinary. Particularly birds. And he paused again before a delicate blue creature which stood on one long brittle leg with its nut-like head cocked under a complicated hat of coloured feathers. This bird did not look at Doole. It stood and jerked its head backwards and forwards, like a little lady in a spring hat practising the neck movements of an Indonesian dance. Doole took out his watch and checked the time. Nearly half an hour before he

need think of the office. Delightful! And what a wholly
delightful day, not a cloud in the golden blue sky! And so
quiet – almost ominously quiet, he thought, imagining for a
moment the uneasy peace of metropolitan parks deserted by
plague or fear. The panic noon, he thought – well, the panic
afternoon, then. Time for sunny ghosts. Extraordinary, too,
how powerful the presence of vegetation grows when one is   70
alone with it! Yet put a few people about the place – all that
power would recede. Man is a gregarious creature, he repeated
to himself, and is frightened to be alone – and how very
charming these zinnias are! How bright, like a consortium of
national flags, the dahlias!

Indeed these colourful flowers shone very brightly in that
September light. Red, yellow, purple and white, the large
flower-moons stared like blodges from a paint box, hard as the
colours of stained-glass windows. The lateness of the year had
dried what green there was about, leaves were shrunken but   80
not yet turned, so that all flowers had a greater prominence,
they stood out as they never could in the full green luxuriance
of spring and summer. And the earth was dry and the gravel
walk dusty. Nothing moved. The flowers stared. The sun bore
steadily down. Such vivid, motionless colour gave a sense of
magic to the path, it did not seem quite real.

Doole passed slowly along by the netted bird-runs, mildly
thankful for the company of their cackling, piping inmates.
Sometimes he stopped and read with interest a little white card
describing the bird's astounding Latin name and its place of   90
origin. A thick-trousered bird with a large pink lump on its
head croaked at Doole, then swung its head back to bury its
whole face in feathers, nibbling furiously with closed eyes. In
the adjoining cage everything looked deserted, old dried
droppings lay scattered, the water bowl was almost dry – and
then he spied a grey bird tucked up on a corner, lizard lids
half-closed, sleeping or resting or simply tired of it all. Doole
felt distress for this bird, it looked so lonely and grieved, he
would far rather be croaked at. He passed on, and came to the

100 peacocks: the flaming blue dazzled him and the little heads
jerked so busily that he smiled again, and turned contentedly
back to the path – when the smile was washed abruptly from
his face. He stood frozen with terror in the warm sunshine.

The broad gravel path, walled in on one side by dahlias, on
the other by cages, stretched yellow with sunlight. A moment
before it had been quite empty. Now, exactly in the centre
and only some thirty feet away, stood a full-maned male
lion.

It stared straight at Doole.

110 Doole stood absolutely still, as still as a man can possibly
stand, but in that first short second, like an immensely efficient
and complicated machine, his eyes and other senses flashed
every detail of the surrounding scene into his consciousness –
he knew instantly that on the right there were high wire
cages, he estimated whether he could pull himself up by his
fingers in the net, he felt the stub ends of his shoes pawing
helplessly beneath; he saw the bright dahlia balls on the left,
he saw behind them a high green hedge, with underbush too
thick to penetrate – it was a ten-foot hedge rising high against
120 the sky, could one leap and plunge half-way through, like a
clown through a circus hoop? And if so, who would follow?
And behind the lion, cutting across the path like a wall, a
further hedge – it hardly mattered what was behind the lion,
though it gave in fact a further sense of impasse. And behind
himself? The path stretched back past all those cages by which
he had strolled at such leisure such a very little time ago – the
thought of it started tears of pity in his eyes – and it was far,
far to run to the little thatched hut that said *Bath Chairs for
Hire*, he felt that if only he could get among those big old safe
130 chairs with their blankets and pillows he would be safe. But he
knew it was too far. Long before he got there those hammer-
strong paws would be on him, his clothes torn and his own red
meat staining the yellow gravel.

At the same time as his animal instinct took all this in, some
other instinct made him stand still, and as still as a rock, instead

of running. Was this, too, an animal sense? Was he, Doole, in his brown suit, like an ostrich that imagines it has fooled its enemy by burying its head in the ground? Or was it rather an educated sense – how many times had he been told that savages and animals can smell fear, one must stand one's 140 ground and face them? In any case, he did this – he stood his ground and stared straight into the large deep eyes of the lion, and as he stared there came over him the awful sense: *This has happened, this is happening to ME.* He had felt it in nightmares, and as a child before going up for a beating – a dreadfully condemned sense, the sense of *no way out*, never, never, and *now*. It was absolute.

The lion, with its alerted head erect, looked very tall. Its mane – and it was so near that he could see how coarse and strong the hair straggled – framed its face hugely. There was 150 something particularly horrible in so much hair making an oval frame. Heavy disgruntled jowls, as big as hams, hung down in folds of muscled flesh buff-grey against the yellow gravel. Its eyes were too big, and from somewhere far back, as far away and deep as the beast's ancient wisdom, the two black pupils flickered at him from inside their lenses of golden-yellow liquid. The legs beneath had a coarse athletic bandiness: the whole creature was heavy and thick with muscle that thumped and rolled when it moved – as suddenly now it did, padding forward only one silent pace. 160

Doole's whole inside was wrenched loose – he felt himself panicked, he wanted to turn and run. But he held on. And a sense of the softness of his flesh overcame him, he felt small and defenceless as a child again.

The lion, large as it was, still had some of the look of a cat – though its heavy disgruntled mouth was downcurved, surly, predatory as any human face with a long upper lip. But the poise of the head had the peculiarly questioning consideration of a cat – it smelled inwards with its eyes, there was the furry presence of a brain, or of a mass of instincts that thought 170 slowly but however slowly always came to the same destined

decision. Also, there was a cat's affronted look in its eyes. A
long way behind, a knobbled tail swung slow and regular as a
clock-pendulum.

Doole prayed: O God, please save me.

And then he thought: if only it could speak, if only like all
these animals in books it could *speak*, then I could tell it how
I'm me and how I must go on living, and about my house and
my showroom just a few streets away over there, over the
180 hedge, and out of the zoo, and all the thousand things that
depend on me and upon which I depend. I could say how I'm
not just meat, I'm a person, a club-member, a goldfish-feeder,
a lover of flowers and detective-stories – and I'll promise to
reduce that profit on fire-surrounds, I promise, from forty to
thirty per cent. I'd have to some day anyway, but I won't
make excuses any more. . . .

His mind drummed through the terrible seconds. But above
all two separate feelings predominated: one, an athletic, almost
youthful alertness – as though he could make his body spring
190 everywhere at once and at superlative speed; the other, an
overpowering knowledge of guilt – and with it the canny hope
that somehow he could bargain his way out, somehow expiate
his wrong and avoid punishment. He had experienced this dual
sensation before at moments in business when he had something to hide, and in some way hid the matter more securely
by confessing half of his culpability. But such agilities were
now magnified enormously, this was life and death, and he
would bargain his life away to make sure of it, he would do
anything and say anything . . . and much the most urgent of
200 his offerings was the promise never, never to do or think
wrong in any way ever again . . .

And the sun bore down yellow and the flowers stared with
their mad colours and the lion stood motionless and hard as a
top-heavy king – as Doole thought of his cool shaded showroom and never, never again would he feel dull there . . .
never again . . .

But it *was* never again, the ever was ever, at any minute

now he would be dead and how long would it take him to die,
how slowly did they tear?

He suddenly screamed.   210

'No!' he screamed. 'No, I can't bear pain! I can't bear it . . .'
and he covered his face with his hands, so that he never saw
the long shudder that ran through the whole length of the
lion's body from head to slowly swinging tail.

In the evening newspapers there were no more than a few
lines about the escape of a lion at the Zoological Gardens.
Oddly – but perhaps no journalist was on the spot and the
authorities wished to make little of it – the story was never
expanded to its proper dimensions. The escape had resulted 220
from a defect in the cage bolting, a chance in a million, and
more than a million, for it involved also a momentary blank
in the keeper's mind, and a piece of blown carton wedged in
a socket, the kind of thing that is never properly known and
never can be explained, and certainly not in a newspaper.
However – the end of it was that the lion had to be shot. It
was too precarious a situation for the use of nets or cages. The
animal had to go. And there the matter ended.

Doole's body was never found – for the lion in fact never 230
sprang at him. It did something which was probably, in a final
evolution over the years, worse for Doole; certainly worse for
his peace of mind, which would have been properly at peace
had his body gone, but which was now left forever afterwards
to suffer from a shock peculiar to the occasion. If we are not
animals, if the human mind is superior to the simple animal
body, then it must be true to say that by not being killed,
Doole finally suffered a greater ill.

For what happened was this – Doole opened very slowly the
fingers that covered his eyes and saw through his tears and the 240
little opening between his fingers, through the same opening
through which in church during prayers he had once spied
on the people near him, on the priest and the altar itself –

he saw the lion slowly turn its head away! He saw it turn its head, in the worn weary way that cats turn from something dull and distasteful, as if the head itself had perceived something too heavy to bear, leaning itself to one side as if a perceptible palpable blow had been felt. And then the animal had turned and plodded off up the path and disappeared at the turn 250 of the hedge.

Doole was left standing alone and unwanted. For a second he felt an unbearable sense of isolation. Alone, of all creatures in the world, he was undesirable.

The next moment he was running away as fast as his legs would carry him, for the lion might easily return, and secondly – a very bad second – the alarm must be given for the safety of others. It was some days before his nerve was partly recovered. But he was never quite the same afterwards. He took to looking at himself for long periods in the mirror. He went 260 to the dentist and had his teeth seen to. He became a regular visitor at a Turkish Bath house, with the vague intention of sweating himself out of himself. And even today, after dusk on summer evenings, his figure may sometimes be seen, in long white running shorts, plodding from shadow to lamplight and again into shadow, among the great tree-hung avenues to the north of Regent's Park, a man keeping fit – or a man running away from something? From himself?

THE AUTHOR

William Sansom (b. 1912) wrote his first book of short stories, *Fireman Flower*, *1944*, about his experiences while serving in the National Fire Service during the bombing of London in the Second World War. Other volumes of stories followed and collected editions appeared in 1963 and 1966. Sansom has also written novels, travel books and children's stories, twenty-five books in all. His latest novel, *Goodbye*, appeared in 1967. He is exceptionally skilled in the use of words and his work is highly praised by his fellow-writers, as well as being enjoyed by the public.

READING NOTES

This is one of Sansom's stories of terror. The only human character is a very ordinary and not particularly attractive man, and there is little action, but our attention is caught in the first few lines and the atmosphere is built up by the description of the zoo, the weather, the time of day and the animals and birds encountered. A crisis is reached, we are made vividly aware of the man's sensations, and then with an ironical twist the terror subsides. Yet our interest is held by the unexpected ending.

Lines 3–4 *most people had . . . on their consciences.* Having enjoyed themselves on Saturday and Sunday, most people would feel guilty if they went to the zoo on Monday.

10 *conformed:* accepted the need to behave like other people.

11 *comportments:* ways of behaving.

15 *writing them off:* dismissing them.

    impracticable: not suitable for carrying out in reality.

18 *brace.* Usually 'braces'.

22–3 *went through:* performed.

29 *paunch.* See page 115, note on line 29.

    baby-fat: rolls of fat like those on a baby's wrists and ankles.

30 *richly sober:* of good quality and dark in colour.

32 *tawny:* light brown.

33 *in fireplaces:* dealing in fireplaces.

37 *like a stuffed dummy:* uselessly.

    while they stuff the real man. They are the people who stay at lunch until three. *Stuff* means 'feed greedily' and *the real man* is contrasted with the *dummy* or doll which has just been mentioned.

40 *dribbling:* hanging down and dripping with blood.

42 *discussing:* considering. The usual meaning of 'discuss' is 'talk about'.

43 *trousered:* covered with thick feathers looking like trousers.

45 *clicked heels:* brought their feet together with a sharp noise.

46 *puss.* Pet name for a cat.

47 *night eyes.* Both owls and cats can see to hunt in the dark.

48 *Likes mice like puss.* The owl, like the cat, likes to eat mice.

50 *come across:* meet.

51 *in the flesh:* in reality.

53 *vase.* Refers to the shape of the owl.

59 *cocked:* turned up to one side.

63 *checked the time:* made sure he knew the exact time.

65 *golden blue.* The description 'golden' is transferred from the sunshine to the sky itself.

67–8 *deserted by plague or fear:* deserted by the people because of plague or fear.

68–9 *The panic noon, he thought – well, the panic afternoon, then.* The ancient Greeks believed that all nature is quiet at midday while Pan, the God of Nature, is resting, and that it is dangerous for men to disturb him. Another old belief is that spirits walk the earth at noon as they do at midnight. ('Time for sunny ghosts', line 69.) The *panic noon* is also the subject of 'The Story of Panic' written by E. M. Forster in 1902 and published in his collected stories.

    well, the panic afternoon, then is 'simply the man's mind fussily regulating the correct time to himself' (W. Sansom). *Well, . . . then* is a phrase used when making a correction in a statement, or accepting a correction made by someone else.

74 *consortium:* gathering. 'Consortium' usually means a partnership between business firms.

80 *what green there was about:* the small amount of green (leaves) still to be seen.

81 *turned:* changed in colour (as in autumn).

84–5 *bore down:* pressed down.

87 *bird-runs:* enclosures for birds.

95 *droppings:* excrement.

96 *lizard lids:* wrinkled eyelids like a lizard's.

112 *flashed:* passed as quickly as a flash of lightning.

116 *net.* The wire-netting of the bird-runs.
    stub: blunt.

117 *dahlia balls:* the rounded heads of a variety of dahlias called 'pompom'.

118 *underbush:* the lower part of the hedge.

124 *impasse:* impenetrability.

127 *started tears:* made tears spring up.

128 *Bath Chairs:* chairs on wheels for the use of invalids.

134 *animal instinct:* instinct which man shares with other animals.

140–1 *stand one's ground:* stand still, not run away from danger.

143 *there came over him:* he experienced.

145 *going up:* going to the teacher. Compare 'going up before a judge'.

152 *disgruntled:* bad-tempered (looking).

jowls: hanging cheeks.

160 *padding:* walking softly like a cat.

161 *wrenched:* torn away violently.

167–9 *The poise of the head had the peculiarly questioning consideration of a cat.* The lion held its head in the special way a cat does when it appears to be thinking and wondering about something.

169 *it smelled inwards with its eyes.* Another, and poetic, description of the lion's thoughtful expression.

furry. A description transferred from its coat to its brain. Compare line 65 'golden blue'.

172 *affronted:* offended. An echo of the mother cat's 'I am affronted' in *The Tale of Tom Kitten* by Beatrix Potter.

173 *knobbled:* with a tuft of hair on the end.

184 *fire-surrounds:* tiled borders round fireplaces.

185 *I'd have to:* I would have to reduce it.

187 *his mind drummed:* his brain throbbed and his thoughts went on inescapably like the beat of a drum.

191 *canny:* cunning.

192 *bargain his way out:* get out by promising something in return.

196 *culpability:* guilt.

197–8 *he would bargain his life away.* This usually means 'he would offer anything, even his life, in exchange for what he wanted'. It is used here ironically, as he is bargaining to save his life.

223 *a piece of blown carton.* A piece of a cardboard box was blown into the hole (socket) where the bolt should slide in, and so the cage could not be closed properly.

227 *precarious:* risky.

234 *had his body gone:* if his body had gone (if he had died).

247–8 *as if a perceptible palpable blow had been felt.* The lion turned its head aside as if it had felt someone actually strike it.

249 *plodded:* walked slowly and heavily.

256 *a very bad second:* far from being first. His thought of saving others comes far behind his desire to escape.

258–9 *took to:* formed the habit of.

260 *seen to:* treated.

262 *sweating himself out.* Doole hoped to get rid of his undesirable characteristics as one 'sweats out' extra weight in a steam bath.

263–4 *long . . . plodding.* Doole is a ridiculous figure. His shorts are too long and he runs heavily and with effort.

264 *from shadow to lamplight.* In suburban streets the street-lamps are widely-spaced and make patches of light with shadows between.

266 *Regent's Park.* The site of the London Zoo.

EXERCISES

A. Answer these questions.

1. Why was the zoo almost empty?
2. Why did Doole like visiting the zoo?
3. What made Doole feel uneasy before he saw the lion?
4. Why did he think he had little chance of escaping?
5. Why did he stand still?
6. What would he have said if the lion could speak?
7. Why was the lion shot?
8. Why was Doole's body never found?
9. How did the lion 'disappear'?
10. What was a greater ill for Doole than being killed?

B. Look through the story and find:

1. evidence that this was a 'fine autumn day';
2. examples of the author's close observation of birds;
3. details of Doole's daily life before the day he met the lion.

C. Find the expressions in the story with the same meaning as those below:

1. near the end of September
2. one who did not obey the general rule
3. a person who does not eat meat
4. scattered carelessly (in)
5. calculated (a number, distance, speed, etc.)

6. making a mark with a coloured liquid
7. deceived its attacker
8. torn away violently
9. make up for his wrong-doing
10. feeling of loneliness

D. Use a phrase with *take* instead of the words in italics in these sentences, and make any necessary changes:

1. He *removed* his watch *from* his pocket.
2. His animal instinct *perceived* all this.
3. How long would *he be occupied in dying*?
4. He *formed the habit of* looking at himself in a mirror.
5. When the ostrich buried its head in the sand its enemy was not *deceived*.
6. The baby was very shy and did not *make friends with* strangers.
7. He *is like* his mother.
8. Doole *became owner and manager of* the business when his father died.
9. When he had got over the shock he *made a hobby of* running.
10. Doole was able to *leave work for an hour* in the afternoon.

E. Complete each sentence to agree with the story by choosing the most suitable of the phrases in brackets.

1. Doole went to the zoo (after his holidays, after his lunch, after his Monday's work).
2. At any moment Doole and the owl might have clicked heels and bowed because (they each had their legs together, Doole was polite to birds and beasts, it was so quiet you could have heard the click).
3. The zoo was almost ominously quiet because (a lion had escaped, there were no people around, the dahlias and zinnias were poisonous).
4. Doole vividly saw every detail of his surroundings (as he walked round the zoo, after standing staring at the lion for a while, at the moment when he saw the lion).

5. Doole's whole inside was wrenched loose because (he was terrified, the lion was tearing him with its claws, he had been beaten at school).

6. He had animal instincts (as a result of visiting the zoo so often, because he was an animal, in his dislike of the sight of red meat).

7. He promised to reduce his profit on fire-surrounds if he (was not attacked by the lion, was forced to do so by his customers, got back to his showroom by three o'clock).

8. He experienced two separate feelings: (a feeling of alertness and the knowledge of guilt, a feeling of guilt and a desire to avoid punishment, a terrible consciousness of life and death).

9. There were no more than a few lines about the incident because (it happened after the evening newspapers had been printed, the zoological society was unwilling to supply details, there were a million lions in the zoo and the loss of one did not matter).

10. Doole felt that he was (the only creature   nobody liked, so lonely that he wished the lion would come back, unattractive only when he was without companions).

F. Subjects for composition and discussion:

1. Write an account of the events in the story as they might appear in a newspaper.

2. Write, or act with a fellow-student, a dialogue between the peacock and his mate about what they saw. Suppose that 'like all those animals in books, they could speak'.

3. Would the story have been more interesting if the lion had attacked Doole? Give reasons for your opinion.

4. Compare Doole's guilty feelings on seeing the lion with the reaction of Belloc's Honest Man on meeting with the Devil.

19

England and Caricature

G. K. CHESTERTON

ENGLISH literature has extracted and emphasised one very
splendid thing; you never hear of it in patriotic speeches or in
books about race or nationality, but it is the great contribution
of the English temperament to the best life of the world. So
far as it can be defined, it may be called the humane use of
caricature. It consists in calling a man ugly as a compliment.
If we wish to appreciate it we must remember the part played
by satire and epigram in the largest part of human literature.
Almost everywhere laughter has been used as a lash; if we
were told about a man's wig or wooden leg, it was done by an 10
enemy. Men reminded a man maliciously of his bodily weakness, especially if it was contrasted with his worldly power.

Take, for instance, the case of two of the greatest riders and
conquerors among the children of men. Julius Caesar was
bald, and he could not cover it all with his laurels. It was
always morally as well as physically his unprotected spot. His
enemies could say: 'You have conquered Gaul, but you are
bald. You have faced Pompey in arms and Cicero in argument,
but for all that you are bald.' And he felt it himself, I think,
for he was a vain man; the head of Caesar was like the heel 20
of Achilles.

Take, again, that huge hunter and fighter who hurled himself on shore at Hastings and created our country by a raid:
William the Norman. If ever a man might have regarded
himself as successful his name was William of Falaise. But in
his later years (like many other great men) he grew rather
stout, and when a Frenchman made a joke about it William

went mad with vanity and violent shame. The mountain shook
to its foundations. He struggled into the saddle, and led a
30 crusade against the Comic Frenchman; shouted like a madman
that he would burn cities and waste provinces to wipe out the
insult, and passing like a pillar of fire at night across the
decaying land, brought his own wild life to an end, was
deserted by all men, died and stank upon the stones.

Such is the power of one really vulgar joke to pull down the
mighty from their seat. And for such purposes it is bitter but
wholesome; it is right that some slave should whisper the
'hominem memento te'. He who seems more than man, ought
to be reminded that he is only man. It should be done, even if
40 it can only be done by telling him that he is less than a man –
less by a leg or so. It is quite right that the poor man who has
no hat should publicly comment on the fact that the rich man
has no hair. But, though it readjusts the balance, it does not
bring about the purest state of feeling. We do not make friends
by pointing out the balance and numbers of glass eyes and
wooden legs in all classes of the community. It produces
equality, but hardly fraternity. And in some literatures it has
become utterly devilish, and men have earned as much shame
by inventing physical epigrams as if they had invented
50 physical tortures.

It is just here, however, that the most characteristic English
literature, from Chaucer to Dickens, has the singular glory. It
is as coarse as any literature; but it is far less malicious than
most. The young fool in *David Copperfield* said that he would
rather 'be knocked down by a man with blood in him than
picked up by a man without'; and understanding 'blood' not as
nobility, but as kindness, I incline to agree with him. Certainly,
if what I wanted was kindness, I would rather be knocked
down by Fielding than picked up by Voltaire. The only really
60 harsh English writer was not English. For Swift was an Irishman, and a very typical Irishman – and like his countryman,
Mr Bernard Shaw, inhuman through the very sincerity of his
humanitarianism. But the point is that this English literary

style, coarse and yet kind, has done more than anything else to create the possibility of a kindly grotesque. As I have said, Julius Caesar was bald and tried to cover his baldness with laurels. But Mr Pickwick was bald and we feel that his head would be spoilt by laurels. Nay, we feel that his head would be spoilt by hair. We like him eternally bald.

Similarly, as I said, William the Conqueror was fat, and furious when reminded of it. But, again, Mr Pickwick was fat; but we do not wish him otherwise. Rather we feel that his roundness is like the roundness of the world; that he is swelling till he takes on the enormous curves of the universe. 'Phiz' dwelt upon the baldness of Pickwick and the fatness of Pickwick because he liked him and them. The satirists of most societies would have insisted on these points as being the weak points of some bad man; but 'Phiz' insists on them as if they were the strong points even of a good one. The French prince called William fat because he had had too much of him. But Dickens made Pickwick fat because you cannot have too much of a good thing. In this matter, however, the pictures of *Pickwick* are even more important than the printed matter. And, indeed, it will commonly be found that the English love of clear comicality for its own sake will be seen better in the old clear, comic illustrations by 'Phiz' and Cruickshank than in any other place. Close your eyes and call up before your mind, say, an old English illustration of an angry admiral with a wooden leg. The wooden leg is insisted on, but not with contempt, and yet, again, not with pity. It is insisted on with enjoyment, as if the Admiral had grown his wooden leg by the pure energy of his character. In any ordinary satire, in any ordinary sentimentality, the point would be that the Admiral had lost a leg. Here it is rather the point that he has gained a wooden leg.

THE AUTHOR

G. K. Chesterton (1874–1936) was a colourful personality in English life and literature in the first half of the twentieth century.

He was educated in London at St Paul's School and at the Slade School of Art. He wrote poetry, both humorous and serious, essays and criticism. He was keenly interested in politics and for some years produced his own paper, *G.K.'s Weekly*. His detective stories, with their amateur detective hero, a Roman Catholic priest called Father Brown, were best-sellers. After his conversion to the Roman Catholic church Chesterton engaged in much religious writing. In his later years he was a well-known figure, enormously fat and usually dressed in a cloak.

READING NOTES

This essay is a mixture of literary and artistic criticism and social history. Chesterton was never afraid of making generalisations and was often prejudiced. He loved to express himself in paradoxes – apparently contradictory statements – and examples occur here. The argument does not develop. Once the theme has been stated it is elaborated in a series of examples.

Line 5 *humane:* not unkind.

6 *caricature:* writing or drawing which distorts its subject.

8 *satire:* art or writing which tries to make its subject ridiculous, often in order to hurt an enemy or correct a social evil.

epigram: a short witty saying or poem.

14 *the children of men:* the human race. A Biblical expression.

15 *laurels.* It is said that Julius Caesar wore a crown of laurel leaves, the symbol of victory, not only to celebrate his triumphs but to hide his baldness.

17 *Gaul.* The Roman name for a region including modern France.

18 *Pompey.* A Roman general defeated by Caesar in 48 B.C.

Cicero. A Roman orator and statesman.

19 *for all that:* in spite of that.

21 *Achilles.* A Greek hero whose mother, according to legend, dipped him in the River Styx. As a result he could not be wounded, except in the heel by which she had held him. The 'heel of Achilles' or 'Achilles' heel' means one's weak spot.

23 *created our country.* This is not historically accurate. The separate kingdoms had already been united, but William established a powerful administration.

24 *William.* William, Duke of Normandy, was born at Falaise.

He invaded England, landing near Hastings in 1066, and became King William I of England usually called William the Conqueror.

30 *Comic.* This usually describes a man who is to be laughed at, but here it describes the Frenchman who laughed at William.

31 *waste:* ruin.

32 *pillar of fire at night.* A Biblical reference to the pillar of fire which is said to have led the Israelites through the desert.

34 *stank:* smelt bad (present tense, *stink*). It refers to William's dead body.

35–6 *pull down the mighty from their seat.* A near-quotation from the Magnificat, the words attributed to Mary, the mother of Jesus Christ, in the Bible.

38 *'hominem memento te':* remember you are only a man. Latin words attributed to a slave speaking to a triumphant Roman general.

41 *less by a leg or so.* This use of 'by' in comparisons states the amount *by* which one thing is different from another. Compare 'greater by far'. 'a leg or so' means 'a leg or more'.

43 *readjusts the balance:* makes things equal.

45 *balance:* proportion.

46–7 *It produces . . . fraternity.* A reference to the motto of the French Republic: Liberty, Equality, Fraternity.

49 *physical epigrams:* jokes about physical deformities.

52 *Chaucer.* English poet (1340–1400). author of *The Canterbury Tales.*

   Dickens. English novelist (1812–70).

   Both Chaucer and Dickens give humorous descriptions of the appearance of their characters.

54 The young fool in *David Copperfield.* A 'simpering young fellow with weak legs' whom Copperfield met at a dinner party, in the novel by Dickens, published 1849–50. In the novel, 'blood' is used to mean 'nobility'.

59 *Fielding.* An English novelist (1701–54), author of *Tom Jones.* He is described by one critic as follows: 'An essentially honest, manly and humane character, he poured contempt on hypocrisy, meanness and vanity.'

   Voltaire. A French philosopher and satirist (1694–1778). He was a critic of the Roman Catholic church. which he accused of intolerance, and a champion of those who suffered persecution.

60 *Swift.* An Irish satirist (1667–1745), and author of *Gulliver's Travels*.

62 *Bernard Shaw.* An Irish dramatist (1856–1950). He was like Chesterton in his fondness for paradox but unlike him in being cynical.

62–3 *inhuman . . . humanitarianism.* A love for the whole human race does not necessarily bring sympathy with the individual.

63–4 *this English literary style*, e.g. that of Chaucer and Dickens.

67 *Mr Pickwick.* The hero of *The Pickwick Papers*, a novel by Dickens, published in 1837.

68 *Nay:* moreover. An old expression.

74 *takes on:* acquires, assumes. For other phrases with 'take' see 'Among the Dahlias', p. 194, Exercise D.
'*Phiz*' (H. K. Browne, 1815–82) and *Cruickshank* (line 86) (1792–1878), illustrators of Dickens' novels.

76 *them:* baldness and fatness.

80 *he had had too much of him:* he was tired of him.

EXERCISES

A. Answer these questions.

1. What writers use caricature kindly?
2. Why do satirists often refer to bodily weakness?
3. How was the head of Caesar like the heel of Achilles?
4. How did William the Conqueror's vanity lead to his death?
5. When is it permissible to remind men of their physical deformities?
6. How does Chesterton feel about being knocked down?
7. Is Mr Pickwick a ridiculous figure? Give reasons for your answer.
8. What is Chesterton's reaction to a picture of an angry admiral with a wooden leg?

B. Look through the essay and find:

1. historical allusions;
2. literary allusions;
3. paradoxes.

C. Complete each sentence to agree with the story by choosing the most suitable of the phrases in brackets.

1. One thing in English literature is very splendid. It is (the part played by epigram and satire, the kindly way of laughing at people, the fact that the English do not boast about their character in patriotic speeches).
2. The largest part of human literature is (satire, not English, done by an enemy).
3. Caesar faced Pompey in arms and Cicero in argument, but (as a result, all that time, in spite of that) he was bald.
4. The result of the Frenchman's joke was that William (was pulled down off his horse, caused his own death, lost his power).
5. In some literatures it has become utterly devilish. This refers to (class hatred, physical torture, physical satire).
6. Chesterton would rather not be picked up by Voltaire because Voltaire was not (kind, noble, English).
7. The artist made Mr Pickwick fat (because he liked his fatness, because Mr Pickwick was bald, because the world is round).
8. The artist made the admiral's wooden leg a symbol of (the energy of the admiral's character, the sentimentality of the English sailor, the contempt we feel for angry people).

D. Find the expressions in the text with the same meaning as those below:

1. the human race
2. victor's wreath
3. towards the end of his life

4. take revenge for
5. made fun of it
6. caused his own death
7. make remarks about, in public

8. cause to happen
9. picture in your imagination
10. for example

E. Rewrite each of the following pairs of sentences as one sentence, using a different expression from this list: *and, as if, because, but, even if, for, if, if ever, so far as, that.*

1. We never make speeches about it. It is our great contribution to the best life of the world.
2. We wish to appreciate human caricature. We must remember the part played by satire in world literature.
3. A man might have regarded himself as successful. That man was William the Conqueror.
4. The proud man must be reminded that he is only a man like other men. It can only be done by laughing at his baldness.
5. Phiz drew Mr Pickwick's bald head. He liked it.
6. The wooden leg is insisted upon. The admiral had grown it by the energy of his character.
7. Caesar was bald. He could not conceal his baldness.
8. William shouted like a madman. He was going to punish the French Prince no matter what destruction he caused.
9. The English contribution can be defined. It may be called the humane use of caricature.
10. Caesar was sensitive to remarks about his baldness. He was a vain man.

F. Subjects for composition and discussion:

1. In what way are Chesterton's language and manner of argument like those of Bertrand Russell ('How to Grow Old', page 74)? In what ways are they different? Which essay do you like best? Why?
2. Give an account of the work of a humorous writer or

artist from your own country or cultural background. In Chesterton's terms is he/she a satirist or a caricaturist?

3. Find a character in one of the stories in this book whom you think the author has made fun of 'because he likes him/her'. Explain your choice with detailed examples from the text.

20

The Collection

V. S. PRITCHETT

IT happens (when it does happen) on Sunday mornings. On weekdays, when he has to go to his factory, he is the first up, but on Sunday mornings he lies in. He awakens and first of all he looks at his wife, who is curled up, with her hair all over her eyes. Typical. What a muddle she makes of sleeping! He turns his face away, looks at the white ceiling and lies there disturbed by the strange silence of the house. That's it; just because it's Sunday and he's not getting up, *they* aren't getting up. Why shouldn't *they* get up for a change?

10   'Edward, Philip, Rose,' he shouts to the children. 'Get up.' And then to his wife, whose wakening eyes glitter like a pair of ants under her hair: 'Come on, girl.'

'Sunday,' he says poetically. 'Look at the sun. It is streaming in. Look at the sky. Listen to the birds. They're not wasting the day.'

But nobody moves.

After this the usual thing happens. It is surprising how no one understands him in the house; he has to lose his temper and start shouting, to get the family to their feet.

20   Downstairs in the kitchen the children are laying the table, kicking the furniture – he can hear that – cleaning his boots.

He is lying in bed, listening to them, when suddenly he remembers:

'Good God, this Sunday I'm taking the collection.'

He is out of bed at once, standing in his pyjamas. Why didn't someone remind him?

The children go to the bottom of the stairs and listen.

'He's in the bath,' they say.

Twenty minutes go by, half an hour, an hour. One after another the children tiptoe and listen.

'He's nearly ready, Mum,' the spy whispers.

He is wearing his tail coat and puts on a silvery tie.

Treading like a cat, floating silkily down, watching the amazing stripes of his trousers, with the gravity of a mourner, he arrives downstairs and pauses in the doorway and puts on the frown he intends to wear as he stands in the chapel waiting for the plate to come down the row. A plate in fact arrives; it is a plate of porridge rushed towards him by his wife.

'Oh,' she cries stopping dead, overturning the plate. 'You give me such a fright.'

'Give!' he says. 'Gave. I'm taking the collection. Am I all right?'

Doesn't she know that it is an important thing to take the collection at the chapel, that people have their eye on you, that it has got to be done properly, and that people say, There's £20-a-week taking the collection? And in a sense, God is looking too. God is saying: That's it. I want the best.

'Give me a brush,' he says. 'Where are those boys? Aren't they coming to church?'

'I don't know where they are,' she says.

'Give the brush to me,' he says.

'They were here,' she says. 'They're outside, I expect.'

'Outside!' he shouts, hitting himself with the brush, working up a rage. 'I don't understand you, outside! The only day their father is home, they're outside . . .'

He bangs the brush down. He is beginning to sweat.

'You'll be late,' she says to him.

'Edward, Philip,' he roars at the door, wiping his hat. There is no answer. 'Come here when I call you.' He puts his hat on. No answer.

'Come and watch your father go. He's going. Come and watch.' She calls in her lighter voice. He stands there waiting, looking as though he will explode.

He has marched off, slamming the gate, as they creep up from the back of the house. The church bells are ringing in the morning heat. No obedience, he thinks (once he is out of the house), no discipline, no love. No religion. No God. No progress. I slave all the week for their education, and what do I get? They bleed you, that's what children do, bleed you white.

70 The Government's the same, bleeds you with taxation. Who goes to church nowadays? No one. Who believes in God – look at the state of the world for the answer. Why did we have a war? Perhaps if it could be reckoned up, if you could get some really good accountant at it, it would turn out that I am the only one who really believes in the Truth. Many think they do; but do they?

And then as he gets near to the granite chapel he is happy. He sees the shabby people go in. They turn to look at him and whisper. Hard, severe, is he? Maybe.

80 He himself goes into the chapel and looks at the small congregation. The believers are few. In the half-empty chapel he gazes at the red brick walls and he is calmed. He rises to sing, he kneels to pray, he sits.

He is awakened by the organ. Before he is ready for it, the time to take the collection has come. On the other side of the aisle he sees Mr Doncaster – wearing an ordinary brown suit – begin his collection as the organ mews and growls like an animal up at the top. He stands up very upright – unlike Mr Doncaster, who is round-shouldered; he puts on the im-

90 personal, official expression – not like Mr Doncaster's, who leans over the congregation thanking them disgustingly like a grocer; he pretends not to hear the chink of coins in the plate and raises his eyes to the roof if there is the rustle of a note. He would like to take Mr Doncaster's side as well, because the pleasure of being given money for nothing has a touch of folly which only a man who has risen in the world can know. And then, as the organ rolls, he and Mr Doncaster walk together, side by side, slowly – he can feel the eyes of the congregation on him, almost heavily on him. He and Mr

Doncaster, like bridegroom and bride, walk up the central aisle; 100
and, after placing their offerings, return with the same gravity.
And all the time he is thinking, Doncaster must feel a fool not
being in black.

The sermon begins. Soon he hears nothing, but he looks
round the chapel. A house with natural oak everywhere is
what he would like, with tall, church-like windows on the
stairs, an organ in the wide entrance hall. Gradually the
chapel turns into a feudal castle, armour everywhere, himself
in a kilt. His wife and children drift about in it, delightful
creatures. Yes, he thinks, they are the children of God. His 110
dreamy eyes come down from the chapel walls and he sees
the yellow bald head of old Doncaster. Yes, he says, poor
old Doncaster who doesn't brush his coat – yes, God made
him, too.

I'm hungry, he says. What an appetite! Going to chapel does
you good. I wonder what there is for lunch?

Unwillingly he leaves the chapel, the scene of his vision.
He arrives at his house. It is at the corner of the street and he
notices that the hedge has not been cut. The boys are tramp-
ling down the garden again. He goes to his high gate. It sticks. 120
He has to shake and rattle and then call. 'Edward! Philip!'
There is no answer. Yet distinctly he heard them. He is obliged
to dirty his gloves and his hands, forcing the gate open. And
what a sight: that paper left on the path.

'Edward,' he says. 'Come here. What's this?'

'Paper, Father.'

Edward's alarmed eyes are fixed on his father's.

'When did you clean your boots?' says the father, sudden in
his attack.

'This morning.'   130

'Don't lie,' says the father. 'Why can't you tell the truth?
A man who doesn't tell the truth, fearlessly, in all circumstances, come what may, loses my trust. If a man lies to me in
my business I sack him – on the spot. Pick that paper up.'

He goes into the house.

'Philip,' he calls. 'Why isn't the table laid? Do you expect your father and mother to slave for you? Don't you know there are no servants? I suppose you think you are a lord or something. Let me tell you, in this world, we are all servants.'

140 He marches into the kitchen. As he advances, he notices a shadow goes with him. Smiles vanish, frowns, lying looks pass over the faces of his family.

His wife is still in her old apron, the sweat from the heat of the fire is on her face as she kneels. He goes out of the kitchen as quickly as he can.

The family are sitting down to lunch.

'Stop kicking the table, Philip,' he says as he carves. He glares. They all lower their eyes.

'Take that plate, pass it down, it's not for yourself. Think of
150 others,' he says. 'Others before self always, the golden rule.' And then he looks at Edward.

'Edward,' he says. 'What have you done to your hair?'

'Nothing.'

'I told you before about lying. Why have you got your best suit on, what's the idea?'

'Edward wants to go out,' says Philip.

'What's that?' he says. 'Your father's only day at home, and you want to go out. I never heard of such a thing.'

The father goes pale as if he had cut himself with the
160 carving knife.

'You stay in and shut up, Edward,' says his mother. 'You cause enough trouble as it is. Get on with your food.'

'Go out with who?' says the father. 'Who is it you value more than your father and mother? It's not some girl, is it? I won't have you go with girls. I don't want trouble with girls at your age. Oh, I'm glad to hear it. You're not telling me lies, are you? You tell lies. I know you deceive me, lie and deceive, but you can't deceive God. He sees. He knows when you're telling lies. I don't like boys who aren't friends with their
170 fathers. It's not some girl? Look me in the face.'

'No,' says Edward in a weak voice. Tears are very near his

eyes. A light glints in the father's eyes. He has seen the son's
weakness.

'N'no, n'no. I don't understand that language. Be straight-
forward. If you mean yes, say yes. If you mean no, say no.
N'n'no. I never heard of it. Sit up straight and speak to your
father. Go on now – what is it?'

Tears pour out of Edward's eyes, tears of rage and shame,
and rush down his cheeks.

'I just want to go out. I want to get away from this,' he 180
shouts, but he is crying so hard that no one understands. He
shouts and cries, starts up and goes out of the room, knocking
his chair over.

'Look what you've done!' shouts his wife, banging down
her knife and fork. 'I can't stand this. Every Sunday the same.
I'm going too.'

And crying also, she leaves the table.

The father stares at the astonishing scene. He looks down
gently at the other children. What on earth have I done? he
silently asks them. He suspects they are going to move too.   190

'Stop where you are,' he says.

He stands there. The food is going cold on his plate. It is all
so astonishing, so sudden. The day he has taken the collection,
too.

Thank God, he thinks, I shall be at the office tomorrow.
People understand me there.

Of course, he gets them back. It takes a bit of doing, the
lunch is cold, but she heats it up again. Everyone has a good
cry, and while they're at it, he goes up and changes into
another suit. Everyone is shy and disappointed and sorry for 200
him after that; and, not to annoy him, no one goes out. They
stay in the room with him, all of them, and in their midst he
falls asleep. He sleeps and sleeps and his snores rise, fall, and
turn over. And waking at last at the end of the afternoon, he
looks at them with surprise. It's all gone, he has forgiven
them.

THE AUTHOR

V. S. Pritchett (b. 1900), who was born in Ipswich, has had a varied career as journalist, novelist, literary critic and broadcaster. He has held lecturing appointments at the Universities of Princeton and Berkeley in the United States. He has a particular talent for short stories in which comic observation of characters brings out the social lessons to be learned from their behaviour. Amongst his best-known works are *Nothing like Leather* (novel), *The Living Novel* (literary criticism) and *When My Girl Comes Home* (short stories).

READING NOTES

'The Collection' describes a day in the life of a lower-middle-class family in England. The day itself is Sunday, which gives the author an excellent opportunity of showing the effect of this particular day on the various members of the family.

Line 3 lies in: stays in bed after the usual time to get up.

24 *taking the collection:* collecting the money offered by the congregation in the chapel. The money is received in a wooden plate.

32 *tail coat:* a coat with long tails (worn on formal occasions).

37 *to come down the row:* to be passed along the row of worshippers.

39 *stopping dead:* stopping completely and suddenly.

39–40 *You give.* Uneducated mistake for 'You gave'.

44 *have their eye on you:* watch you critically.

45–6 *there's £20-a-week:* there's a man earning £20-a-week (a good wage at the time the story was written).

46 *in a sense:* in a metaphorical sense. He makes a difference between the way the congregation looks at him and the way, God 'sees' him.

48 *Give me a brush:* i.e. a clothes brush. The children have already cleaned his shoes.

58 *wiping his hat.* The father wears a top hat which has to be smoothed each time it is worn. A top hat is always worn with a tail coat.

68 *I slave:* I work like a slave.

69 *bleed you white:* take everything they can get from you.

74 *turn out:* appear, be discovered.

79 *Hard, severe . . .* This is what he likes to imagine the poor people are saying about him.

88 *at the top:* at the end of the chapel where the minister stands.

94 *to take Mr Doncaster's side:* to take the collection on Mr Doncaster's side of the chapel.

120 *it sticks:* it refuses to open.

133 *come what may:* regardless of the consequences, whatever may happen.

134 *I sack him – on the spot:* I dismiss him at once.

147 *carves:* cuts the meat into slices. In many English families a large piece of roast meat is served on Sundays, and this is carved by the father in the dining-room.

158 *I never heard of such a thing.* I strongly disapprove of it.

161 *shut up:* be quiet (slang).

165 *I won't have you go:* I won't allow you to go.

170 *look me in the face:* look straight at me.

197 *it takes a bit of doing:* it is quite difficult (to persuade all the family to return to the dining-room).

EXERCISES

A. Answer these questions.

1. Why does the father get up first on weekdays?
2. What makes the family get up on this Sunday?
3. What makes the father get on this Sunday?
4. Why does the mother spill the porridge?
5. What is wrong with Mr Doncaster in the father's eyes?
6. How does the father occupy himself during the sermon?
7. What has his wife been doing while he was at Chapel?
8. Why is he angry with Edward at lunch?
9. Why does the mother leave the table?
10. How does the father spend this Sunday afternoon?

B. Imagine that you are giving instructions to an artist who is to illustrate the story. Describe in as much detail as possible:

1. the Father; 2. the Chapel; 3. the scene in the kitchen, at breakfast time *or* before lunch.

C. There are several examples in this story of a common English construction: a verb telling us the *kind* of action done, followed by a word telling us the *direction* in which the action moved or its *effect* on its object. e.g. *He floated* (kind of action) *down* (direction of action). *He banged* (kind of action) *down the brush* (effect on the brush – it was put down). Find in the story a construction like this with the same meaning as each of the expressions below:

1. coming in freely
2. (a plate) carried towards him in a hurry
3. approach very quietly
4. running about the garden in a way that flattens the plants
5. enters with a firm decisive step
6. come out like water from a jug
7. fall down very fast
8. pushing his chair so that it falls on its side
9. putting down her knife with a loud noise
10. persuades them to return

D. 1. Rewrite 'He awakens' (line 3)... 'remind him?' (line 26) using *I* instead of *he* for the father, telling the story in the past and making other necessary changes.
   2. Rewrite 'He goes to his high gate' (line 120) . . . 'This morning.' (line 130) as if Edward was telling it. Use past tenses and reported speech. Begin *Father came to our high gate* . . .

E. Expand these exclamations and incomplete sentences into whole sentences.

Example

Give! Gave (line 41). Don't say 'give'. It should be 'gave'.

1. Typical (line 5).
2. no answer (line 60).
3. No obedience . . . no discipline, no love (lines 66–7).

4. Maybe (line 79).
5. What an appetite! (line 115)
6. And what a sight: that paper left on the path (lines 123–4).
7. Paper, Father (line 126).
8. This morning (line 150).
9. Others before self always, the golden rule (line 150).
10. Every Sunday the same (line 185).

F. Find sentences in the text with the same meaning as those below.

1. They are making good use of the day.
2. He has to get angry to make the family get up.
3. Am I correctly dressed?
4. God can be said to be looking, too.
5. I work hard all the week to pay for the children's education.
6. The children take all your money.
7. There are not many people in the congregation. .
8. The organ makes squeaky and deep noises.
9. He knows the people in the Chapel are watching him.
10. It's difficult to do.

G. Subjects for composition and discussion:

1. You are Philip or Rose. Tell a school friend what happened at Sunday lunch.
2. What impressions would you form about an English Sunday from reading this story?
3. Write character sketches of the father as seen by (a) his wife, (b) himself, (c) the people at the Chapel.
4. Compare the authors' treatment of the father, Pyecraft ('The Truth About Pyecraft', page 164) and Walter Mitty ('The Secret Life of Walter Mitty', page 81). Which of the men do you feel you know best? Why?